As I Was Saying ...

Cliff Dochterman

President of Rotary International,
1992-93

A Collection of Favorite Speeches and Articles

Printed in the United States of America
By Booksurge, Charleston, South Carolina

ISBN: 1-4392-5027-8
ISBN 13: 9781439250273
LCCN: 2009909938

Visit www.booksurge.com to order additional copies.

As I Was Saying...

A Collection of Favorite Speeches and Articles

By

Cliff Dochterman
President, Rotary International
1992-93

WHY PUBLISH THIS BOOK?

For over fifty years, I have spoken to hundreds of Rotary Clubs, civic organizations, university audiences, and community groups. There has been a pleasure in sharing ideas, motivating audiences, and often merely providing a moment of entertainment. These activities have been purely a "labor of love" and the use of a talent, which I have tried to cultivate from early school days.

Frequently, I have been asked to give copies of speeches to interested friends or listeners. I have generally refrained from distributing copies of manuscripts or addresses, because each presentation was designed for presentation in the style of the writer and seldom have they had the same impact when imitated or repeated by others. Now, that I am reaching the autumn years, many Rotarian friends have urged that I share in printed form some of the presentations and experiences which have been the cornerstone of my speaking career. This collection largely relates to the many Rotary audiences which I have addressed.

The reader will find that there are often similar themes or even a few stories which have been repeated in different presentations throughout the book. To delete segments of a speech merely because they may have been used in other addresses would unduly compromise the continuity and consistency which most speeches should contain. Some of these speeches have been prepared over a 25 year period, so many of the dates and figures may be accurate as of the date when the speech was original written.

It is in this spirit that I present in print, a number of my favorite platform presentations and a selection of short articles which I call, Presidential Minutes.

Cliff Dochterman

TABLE OF CONTENTS

ACKNOWLEDGMENTS

It is fitting that I should express my grateful appreciation to the hundreds of Rotary Clubs and other groups which have so generously invited me to tell some of the stories about my Rotary experiences and to encourage Rotarians to discover the values of friendship and service. Except for a few occasions, all of these events have been very enjoyable and personally rewarding. Without those Rotary lunches, dinners, conferences, institutes and other occasions, these speeches would never have been written.

My wife, Mary Elena, also deserves special acknowledgment, not only for proofreading these manuscripts; but, also for sitting through an almost endless array of speeches so many times that she could always tell if I added a new story or left one out. My son, Cliff, and Karen Wetherell have provided a huge contribution to the publication by handling the computer technology which transformed all of the basic documents into a copy format.

I must also say, "Thank you very much!" to the several Past Presidents of Rotary International, whose generous comments are on the back cover. Each of these Rotary friends is well familiar with the many speaking demands upon a Rotarian who has been given the rare privilege to lead the worldwide Rotary organization.

IF I COULD BE CLUB PRESIDENT AGAIN

[Of all the speeches I have given, this one seems to be the most popular. It has been presented to over 125 President Elect Training Seminars throughout the United States over 25 years, and recorded on video and DVDs]

As I look around and see all of this Rotary brass, I realize that Rotarians come and go – but District Governors just accumulate. I remember my first contact with a Rotary Governor. I was a brand new Rotarian attending my first District Conference up at a big hotel in Sacramento, California. It was just at the time the hotel had taken the paper towels out of the rest rooms and installed those warm air machines. Sure enough, during the conference, I went into the rest room to wash my hands. There was a small card Scotch taped above the hot air machine. It said, "Push the button and hear a short message from the District Governor."

We occasionally joke about District Governors, but they are fantastic Rotarians who generously give their time and talent. We appreciate and love them. Kind of like a favorite pair of old tennis shoes – all worn out, except the tongue.

IF I COULD BE PRESIDENT AGAIN

To prepare these remarks today, I visited former Rotary club presidents in rest homes and sanitariums up and down the Pacific Coast. It was a thrilling sight to see those past presidents just lying there being waited on hand and foot. As they clutched the coverlets, they all agreed that there will be room for each of you when your time comes. And it will come a heck of a lot faster than you may think.

Oh, I'll never forget my first day as a Rotary club president. I remember I stepped up to the rostrum, grabbed the gavel in my right hand and the bell in my left hand and wham – sure enough, I missed the bell and broke the index finger on my left hand. From then on, my year kind of went down hill. I think I had one of those years where you start slow – then taper off.

Being club President is the greatest job in Rotary – next to assistant bulletin editor. Every week you learn a lot about Rotary. So I kept a list of the things I learned. I brought some the lists along today to share with you – of just what I learned week after week as a Rotary club president. This first list is the one I prepared at the end of my first month as club president. These are the things I wrote:

1.   The club president has an almost impossible chance of being an early leaver.

2.   That first meeting of the year will give you a brand new feeling – kind of a sickness in the pit of your stomach.

3.   It is important to keep the fingers of the left hand off the bell when you have the gavel in your right hand.

4

4.   The club secretary is supposed to do all the work.

5.   A speaker on artificial insemination is not a good program for ladies day.

6.   The first law of a Rotary club president is: "Whatever hits the fan will never be distributed evenly."

7.   A Rotarian is a person who can find 27 different classifications in the banking industry.

8.   It is best not to preside at your club meetings – under heavy sedation.

9.   Rotarian lunches are a thing of beauty – it's the only place a person will pay fifteen dollars for a peanut butter sandwich.   In our club, we were always trying to get the price of the lunch as low as the quality of the food.

10.   Every District Governor will suggest at least one scheme which doesn't work – and that will be the one you try in your club.   During my year, the club presidents had some disagreements with the Governor on religious differences – he thought he was God, and we didn't.

Well, that was my first month Three months went by, and I learned more and more about Rotary. So, I made up another list:

1.   The club secretary does not necessarily do all the work.

2.   Fining the District Governor ten dollars on his or her annual visit is not the Governor's idea of fun. Just

remember, of all the 530 District Governors in the world – half of them are below average.

3. My club directors always approached a new project in a three-step procedure – READY, FIRE, AIM.

4. You can sleep undetected during the speech by resting your head on your hand, as if shading your eyes. (Like a couple of you folks are doing there in the back of the room.)

5. It's good to emphasize the Four-Way Test. But, our club was so small we only had a 3-Way Test. We had those three questions, of course – Is it fun? Will it hurt anyone? And, Will anyone find out?

6. We had a community service project too. Our motto was, "Don't worry about crime in the streets – just get it off the sidewalks." We sent kids to summer camp – even when they didn't want to go.

7. One of the most intriguing talks of my year was called "General Custer is alive and well in Argentina." I remember one day we had a speaker who spoke about the Jimmy Carter Library, and the Ronald Regan Library, the Gerald Ford Library and the Bill Clinton Adult Bookstore.

8. A Rotarian is a person who will drive 56 miles to a make-up meeting – and then leave before the program begins.

9. A club project not worth doing, is not worth doing well.

10. You should learn that before you criticize someone, walk a mile in his shoes -- at least he'll be a mile away and barefoot.

Well, the year slowly crept on, and by January I became confident and self-assured; and I continued to learn other things about Rotary. Here is the list I made up along with my New Year's resolutions:

1.   You wonder what the heck the club secretary really does. You learn the first rule for club secretaries is – "When you don't know what you are doing, always do it neatly."

2.   There is practically no non-violent way to stop a speaker who has gone past I: 30.

3.   A $25 fine doesn't always build better friendships.

4.   It is not too good an idea to schedule a pacifist to speak at your club meeting -- especially on Veterans Day.

5.   Remember, the District Governor is the person you call in at the last minute to share the blame. That's when you begin to realize how some Governors have real delusions of adequacy.

6.   The club president will find that the community service   committee doesn't always follow the President's suggestions.

7.   The club directors do not always follow the President's suggestions.

8.   Nobody seems to follow the President's suggestions.

9.   The club president is supposed to remember the R.I. President's theme. In my year the theme was "Honk If You Love Paul Harris."

10.   One of the most intriguing programs of my year was a talk by the Chief of Police on the subject of prostitution – he called the subject, "It takes a Heap of Loving to Make a Home a House." Oh, we had some great programs during my year. I recall one program – "Penicillin – The Gift for the Man who has Everything." We had Dr. Kevorkian give a motivational speech, and Judge Judy spoke on brotherhood week. We had speakers on: "Brain Surgery for Fun and Profit;" "Home Tattooing by Numbers;"   and "Can a Woman 65 Find Happiness with a Man Twice Her Age?" That is just an idea of the wealth of information you can pick up week after week at a Rotary club meeting. Oh, I remember one fascinating program. We had an armless sculptor. He held the chisel in his mouth and his wife hit him on the back of the head with a mallet. In some clubs, a committee evaluates their weekly programs. If the District Governor's visit was voted the best program of the year, you probably need a new program chairman.

Well, no matter what you think, your year will come to an end. By then the club President's knowledge is nearly complete. Here is the list I prepared in those waning days of my year:

1.   It is important to keep the fingers of the left hand off the bell when you have the gavel in your right hand.

2.   A District Governor is the kind of person who is always around when he needs you. Most District Governors have friends they haven't even used yet.

3.   Club presidents are supposed to uphold the classification system – whether they understand it or not. The description of our classifications is always a

fascinating subject. I have a friend in the New York Rotary Club with the classification of "diamond cutter" – he mows the lawn at Yankee Stadium

4.   Every Rotary Club has a pessimist and an optimist. A pessimist is the guy who wears belt and suspenders at the same time. And the optimist is the fellow who gets married at the age of 70 and looks for a home near a school.

5.   Your International Service program ought to be more than setting up a Chrysler dealership in Tokyo.

6.   Rotarians like to hear speakers every week – but they only have an attention span of 5 minutes – and that isn't consecutive.

7.   Vocational Service talks by the local undertaker should be avoided – even if the subject is "How to Look Sad at a $30,000 Funeral."

8.   You learn that Rotarians are not old – just mature. I wouldn't say the members of my club are old – but our club lunches are catered by Meals on Wheels. We have a Breakfast Club – which meets at noon. We have a few older members in my club. Why do they think Rotarians are so old – one guy in my club bragged that he made love for an hour and three minutes? When was that? The night they turned the clocks back. The other day I asked my wife: "Do I really look 80?" She said, "No... but you used to." The guys in our club are so old, the insurance agent in the club who gives out calendars each year to our members – only gives 3 months at a time.

9.   At our district conference, we received a district award for our club's literacy program – we smuggled books into Texas.

10.   Finally, the last meeting of your year will give you another brand new feeling – but this time it is not a sickness in your stomach; it is a sickness in your heart – because you will have just ended one of the grandest years of your life.

Well, I had better say something before I finish.

I bet the one common goal in this room is that you are looking for success!   Success as a club president! Success for your Club!   But stop – take a look at your hands. The success of your club is entirely in your hands.   Most club presidents start out their year with the president's prayer – "Dear God, don't let the club fall apart during my year!"

It need not fall apart — it can be the best year your club has ever seen. The success of Rotary is in the hands of the 33,000 club presidents around the world. And it's in your hands – because you are the President – you are the leader!

There is hardly a past club president who hasn't said, "Oh, if I could do it all over again, I'd have done a better job for my club. Oh, if I were club president again, I'll tell you what I would do.

The first thing I would do if I could be president again would be to insist upon better weekly meetings. A Rotary meeting must be fun. It must be enjoyable, if you want your members to be there every week.   Good programs are the best insurance for retaining high club membership, maintaining regular attendance and eliminating the 'early leaver' problem. Of course, every meeting can't be a weekly production of the comedy club or an extravaganza to rival the Super Bowl. But you have to have an interesting meeting each week if you want to retain your membership. People want to join a club which is alive and fun to attend. Your program committee can be the most important in your club. The weekly meetings are the only part of Rotary most members ever see. Members should look forward to attending the meetings as a highlight of their week.

I'd spend more time on the care and feeding of our speakers. I'm ashamed how poorly most Rotary clubs treat their guest speakers by the thoughtless lack of common courtesy, or even a note of thanks. Do you reserve a parking space for the speaker? Is there someone who greets the speaker? Is the speaker introduced around to the club members? Think how poorly we frequently introduce the speaker. The introduction sets the stage for the speaker to do his or her best job. And think how seldom our members even bother to go up afterwards and say "thanks" for coming to our club and giving your time. Time after time, the club president or a sergeant-at-arms takes the speaker's time by fooling around, or just poor planning. Don't steal the speaker's time any more than you would steal their wallet. Most speakers have a prepared message and can't be turned on and off like a garden hose.

Then take a look at your rostrum. Does it have a light, which works? Does the PA system operate properly? Get one of the talented members of your club to build a new first-class rostrum for your club. Does your club banner on the wall look like a distress signal? The atmosphere of the meeting room can actually influence the success of your weekly meetings. I'd never permit empty tables in the front of the room – they are discourteous to your speaker and make it more difficult for any speaker to do their best job.

Then I would provide a small gift for each speaker. It might be a product from your local community or a symbol of Rotary. In these days with high gasoline prices, consider an additional gift card for a tank or two or gas, if your speaker has driven a substantial distance to your meeting. The value of the gift is not nearly as important as the thought of gratitude to our guests who gave their time and energy so graciously – just to entertain and inform your club.

I'd take a look at the 20 or 25 minutes I have as president to conduct the business at each meeting. I'd make good use of those vital minutes, and not just follow the way other presidents did it in the past. If I needed more time – I'd just start earlier. Seldom does any Rotary program run over because of what was on the end of the program – they run over because of extra things put in at the beginning – or just a failure to start early enough. I've attended meetings so bad that I've thought, I think I'll slip out the back door – then I realize I'm the speaker.

When we introduce our visitors, I'd make it alive, sincere and fun. The introduction of guests is one of the most important and unique parts of a Rotary club meeting -- because it expresses the worldwide fellowship of Rotary. A Rotarian is privileged to walk into any Rotary club meeting in the world. So, make those introductions as warm and friendly as you would if introducing a guest in your home or office.

Oh, if I could do it all over again, I'd never give encouragement to early leavers by saying, "It's now time for early leavers to leave." I would not allow my club to be disrupted by the thoughtless and discourteous Rotarians who have the habit of walking out just as the speaker is introduced.

If I were club president again, at every meeting we would have some interesting Rotary information about our fascinating history and traditions, or a committee report on our service programs. Throughout the year, I'd have some of the past club presidents give a 3 minute report on the big event of their year. I might even have a short Presidential Minute each week to give a little Rotary message or maybe even use that informational booklet, the ABC's of Rotary.

Oh, if I could be president again, I'd do everything I could to make my meetings come alive! I've come to the conclusion that one of the biggest reasons for the drop in membership or poor attendance is that club meetings just aren't fun, interesting, and worth attending.

The second thing I would do would make my Rotary club relevant to the community, the world and to the lives of our club members. Service is our reason for existing. I've seen clubs where their only service activity is an annual gift to the Tennis Elbow Foundation. Once in a while they give a check to The Society to Protect Azaleas During Nuclear Attack. They attend the Cheerleaders car wash and support the Boy Scouts' pumpkin sale and think they have done enough in their community. And they call it a service club.

Far too many Rotary Clubs have no program of hands-on service at all – except the activity of writing checks to other groups. You can drive down most highways of our country and never know that a Rotary Club exists – except for the aging sign that tells where Rotary goes to lunch.

Take a hard look around any city and there are *hand-on jobs* to do. I don't think there is a single community where we can't find people who are hungry or homeless, or problems of drugs and substance abuse, or schools or community recreation facilities, which need repair improvement or expansion.

So, my plea is that if your Rotary club is to be relevant in the world today and into the 2lst Century, it must be addressing some real problems of your community. Rotary check writing is no substitute for hands-on community service. A great club does both! If you want busy people to join your Rotary club – you have to be doing something which merits their time and attention! Everyone needs a worthwhile job, which is building a better community.

If I could be club president again, we would create a Rotary image. We'd build the Rotary playground, the Rotary drug prevention program, some Rotary shelters, the Rotary food bank, or Rotary youth center. We'd show the community that Rotary is alive and well in our town. Frankly, I'm tired of seeing Rotary clubs being the finance or fund raising committee for every other group in town, without Rotary ever getting an ounce of recognition – and we wonder why nobody knows what a Rotary club does.

Oh, if I could be president again, I would insist that our Rotary club have its *own* programs of service – and we would let the community know that Rotary is an organization of doers. We might even get some fantastic Rotary billboards to show the image of Rotary.

Do you see the point I am trying to make? If Rotary is going to be relevant – if Rotary is going to be attractive to busy and committed young business and professional executives, we have to have the courage to face the problems of the urban areas in the 21st Century – and get involved! Community leaders must say, "I want to be a part of that Rotary club."

Now, the final step in my second time around would be to make more plans than I ever thought possible. To have a successful year, you have to set some goals and then strive to achieve them. You are the key person who will determine where your club will be on June 30th next year!

Sure, you have to involve your Club's directors – but you must take the lead. I'd know where we were going and when we arrived. Your goals must be written and shared with your club. Put them on a poster and hang them on the wall – print them frequently in your club bulletin. Talk about them at every meeting. Remember that great philosopher, Yogi Berra, said: "IF YOU DON'T KNOW WHERE YOU ARE GOING – YOU'RE LIABLE TO END UP SOMEPLACE ELSE."

Oh, if I could lead my club again, I'd have a new goal for our vocational service and community service activities. I'd have a goal for a new international service project and seek a matching grant from the Rotary

Foundation, and a goal for Paul Harris Fellows. I'd make plans now for our fellowship events, social activities and participation in the district conference. I'd put those dates on the calendar right now. I'd know how many members we were seeking and how they would be indoctrinated into the spirit of Rotary.

You see, if *you* don't have a specific measurable goal for each area of Rotary activity, you will never know whether your Rotary club achieves success or not in your year. I'd print the goals. I'd hang them above the head table. I'd talk about them. I'd measure our progress every month. I'd show what we have accomplished and what we have yet to achieve. And the amazing thing is that your club members will take pride in *their success!*

My friends, there isn't a Rotary club in the world which can't be improved. Oh, if I had the honor of leading my club again, I'd say: "Yes, we can be a better club!" And would you believe it – it's all within your grasp, because you're the President.

Well, those are the things I'd do if I could be club President again – and on the seventh day I'd rest!

Fellow, Rotarians, you've been *selected to lead* your Rotary club next year – it is a responsibility not to be taken lightly. Your club will always remember your year – one way or another. Make it one you'll be proud to recall. If there is anything in this message, it is simply this: *You don't have to do it just as it has always been done. You must believe that you can do it better.*

Don't worry about occasional thoughtless criticism, or the foot-draggers in your club. Don't listen to the old past presidents or past governors who caution that, "We never did it that way before." Just remember, when the parade of success begins, everyone will want to be on your bandwagon. And they will all be saying, "*We sure had a great year!*"

So, as I shuffle off into the sunset, just remember that few of you will ever be called again to lead your Rotary club as you have been called for next year. For most club presidents, the opportunity only knocks once. Make the best of your opportunity, and you will not have to think back wistfully some day and say, "If I could only be President again..."

So, go to it!

YOU CAN CHANGE THE LIFE FOR SOMEONE

(This speech, with some variations, has been given to many Rotary clubs at weekly meetings. It was intended to encourage Rotarians to see that service can be a very personal activity as well as a club activity.)

This year, I completed 50 years of attending Rotary meetings. A friend asked me, "Why do you Rotarians feel that they have to attend meetings every week?" My answer was: "Well, you just never know who needs you."

As I look around this room, I see so many of you who have been great friends for many years. You have been brought together by the magic of a Rotary club.

Do you realize how important it is that you come to Rotary each week if it is at all possible? Did you ever stop to think that there might be someone in this room who really needs you? You never know who is troubled, whose life is in despair, or who is going through a tough time – and the friendship you find at Rotary could really make a difference.

Nearly everyone you meet at Rotary is fighting some kind of battle in their personal, family or business affairs. A pat on the back, a warm handshake, a listening ear, a friendly comment, – all of these acts of friendship could make a huge difference in someone else's life. On the other hand, there might be someone who is bursting with pride or excitement and needs someone to share his or her good fortune. And the amazing thing is – you may never know what your presence or friendship can mean when you walk into your Rotary meeting.

I recall giving a speech in Oakland some years ago. I talked about tramping through the mud huts of an African village giving polio vaccine. I mentioned that if our little group hadn't been in that remote village, there probably would be no one in the world who really cared about those poverty stricken youngsters.

When the luncheon was over, a Rotarian came up to me with a young lady, who had been his guest. He said she would like to speak to me. Then she said, "I am a school teacher in one of the toughest high schools in the inner city of Oakland. My work is so difficult and I have been planning to resign from teaching. But listening to you today, I made up my mind – those kids need me." Tears came to her eyes. She continued, "I made up my mind that I'm going to continue to be an inner city teacher, no matter how tough it gets. Thanks for helping me see what my job really is, and that someone needs me."

You see, you never know which person in the audience is ready to hear the message of service to others. You never know who needs your friendship when you walk into a Rotary meeting.

I remember speaking in Seattle in the early days of the Polio Plus program. After the lunch, a Rotarian came up to the lectern and handed me a check for $1000. He said, "I want to be one of those Paul Harris Fellow things. Today I discovered what the Rotary Foundation really does. I had polio as a child and that's why I've walked with this cane all my life. It would mean a lot to me if I could prevent just a few other children from following my crippled footsteps. Maybe I could change the life of someone."

That's the amazing message of Rotary. Maybe I could change the life for someone. Or, maybe working together, we could change the world for everyone.

That great philosopher, physician and African missionary, Dr. Albert Schweitzer said it this way. "I do not know what your destiny will be: but this I do know, the only ones who will find true happiness in life, are those who have searched and found how to serve others."

In Rotary you never know what one person can do to help others.

Ernst Ragg was a Rotarian in Austria who was selected to be Governor of his Rotary District during the year that I was RI President. It wasn't going to be too big of a job – visit the clubs, make a few speeches, write the reports – and then be Past District Governor forever. Well a civil war broke out in nearby Bosnia and Croatia, and the Rotarians in Austria and Germany began to help the fleeing refugees. All of a sudden, Ernst Ragg, just a common Rotarian like you or me, was in the middle of a huge humanitarian relief effort. He sent me a letter to the RI President's office in Evanston. He said, we are doing all we can to help the refugees. Is there anything that the Rotarians of the world could do to help? He had a postscript on his letter, "If you can't help, I'll understand, but pleased do not appoint a committee."

I wanted to make sure that any help we would give would not be stolen in the black market or confiscated by the military. So, I flew to Austria, and Ernst and a few other Rotarians flew with me to Croatia – I might add, on a little plane called "Air Croatia," if I remember correctly. With the security protection of United Nations forces, we visited several of the refugee camps, where Rotary was assisting with food, clothing, blankets, medicines and any other help they could give. It was so sad to see these people, old folks and little kids, who had nothing but what they could carry – and dependent upon what others were able to give them.

I recall one little incident when I was in Zagreb, Croatia. A newspaper reporter was interviewing me. He asked, "Who are you helping, the Bosnians, Croatians, Muslins, or Serbians?" I answered, "Frankly, I don't know. We are helping children and people in need. Rotary doesn't ask about their religion, nationality or ethnic background – Rotary helps where the need exists."

After returning from Bosnia, I sent out a letter to the Rotary District Governors asking for help. In a matter of 5 weeks, the money poured in, airplanes loaded with supplies came from Canada, trucks loaded with food and warm clothing arrived from all over Europe.

One little Rotary Club in Zagreb, Croatia coordinated the delivery to about 34 refugee camps each day. German Rotarians packed 10 Mercedes vans and drove them all the way to Croatia and gave the vans and contents to the Zagreb Rotarians to use to deliver goods to the refugees. It was estimated that over 8 million dollars worth of money and donated goods were delivered in that relief effort – all started by one Rotarian – who made a difference in the lives of others.

The United Nations reported to me that this effort alone saved the lives of over 100,000 people from freezing or starving to death in that deadly civil war. It is amazing what one person can do.

I recall a statement made by that great woman, Helen Keller, who accomplished so much in her lifetime. She said: "I always dreamed of performing some great and noble tasks. But I am destined to perform just small and humble tasks, as if they were great and noble."

Few of us are able to save the lives of war-torn refugees, or create a cure for cancer, or build schools in Afghanistan, or perform cleft palate surgery in South America or deliver wheelchairs in developing nations. Most of us do not have the ability to perform surgery to change the lives of hundreds of people in Africa.

But, let us not forget that every Rotary activity is not world shaking or monumental. Actually, most of the service tasks we are destined to perform are small and humble. But that doesn't mean they should not be done. Building a better community right here where you live – that is a noble task. Teaching a person to read is a noble task. Caring for those who are sick is a noble task. Organizing a drug and substance abuse prevention program for kids of the community is a noble task. Taking food to a food bank or a mission dining room is a noble task – not just on Holidays, but any day. Listening to a friend or giving encouragement to a fellow Rotarian, could be a priceless gift greater than you could ever imagine.

As I traveled the world, I watched individual Rotarians give their greatest gift – their time and personal efforts – to meet the needs of those who live in poverty, hopelessness or just facing despair.

In Malaysia, I distributed shoes to school children who had no shoes. In the Philippines, I passed out eyeglasses and worm medicine to youngsters who lived in deep pockets of poverty. In Mexico, one day I delivered bags of food from the back of a pick-up truck to hungry people in Tampico. These are just common things – but they make a real difference in the lives of others.

In every community, there are small tasks that become great and noble. It is amazing what you personally can do in someone else's life. Reading a book to kindergarten or first grade classes could be a gift to youngsters who have never heard an adult read stories. In 10 minutes, you could be their hero.

Have you ever visited a senior center, and spent an afternoon talking, laughing and listening to people who have no one with whom to talk? You would be amazed at how important an hour could be.

Have you ever gone to the store and loaded your car trunk with canned food and taken it all to the local food bank? And see the surprise on their faces when you show up and it isn't even a special holiday.

What I am saying is that Rotary Service can be little acts of kindness and caring. I'll tell you doing just little random acts of kindness are a fantastic project for a Rotary club. Your President might ask what "acts of kindness" each member performed when you meet next week. Just random acts of kindness could change a community – or if not – doing nice things for others, will scare them out of their mind!

My message is simply this. For Rotary service to be important, you do not have to be President of Rotary International, or District Governor, or even Club President. *Service Above Self* is our motto. Service for others can happen every day. Just little acts of kind and thoughtful service – for your neighbors, customers, youth groups, senior centers, employees, and others with whom you deal every day. That's what Rotary's motto is all about – *Service Above Self.* The very thought that you walk into this Rotary club meeting room each week, could be a kind of service to someone in a way you will never know.

There is so much more to being a Rotarian than meeting, eating, singing, having fun and enjoying the friendship of a great group of friends and then going back to work or playing golf. Being a Rotarian gives us opportunities to touch the lives of people we may never know, or build a better community where we live, or even reach out to those around the world whom we will never meet or ever see.

In this small world, the lives of all of us are woven together. That is why Rotarians reach out to people that they may never know or ever meet, and serve in ways they may never imagine.

You would be surprised how many people need you, and what small, random acts of kindness can do to make a difference in the lives of others. Never under-estimate the power of your smile, a hug, a handshake, a kind word, a sincere compliment, a listening ear, or the smallest act of caring – all of which have the potential to make a difference. People come into our lives for a reason, for a season, or for a lifetime.

Can you believe it – *you* can change the life of some-one. And it can happen right here, once a week, and can be continued every day – just because you are a Rotarian.

FRIENDLY FIRE OF ROTARY

(This speech was originally prepared in 2007 for several "membership seminars" established by the President of Rotary International. It was subsequently presented at several Rotary clubs and conferences as well as recorded and distributed on a DVD.)

Rotary International recently published the worldwide membership trends. North America is the one place where we see a slight downward slide. In the last 5 years, there was a decrease of nearly 16,000 members in the North American Rotary clubs. In the same 5-year period, Europe and Africa had an increase of a little over 15,000 new members.

What could be causing this slow decline in Rotary membership in North America and yet an increase in Europe and other areas? Are there negative stories about Rotary being told by the media? No. Is there some anti-service club movement? No. Are Rotary clubs less important in North America than in Europe? No, I don't think so. Just, what is causing this slight downward trend?

It came to me one evening as I watched a television broadcast. The evening television news showed a story of two Army officers who were delivering the tragic news of the death of the family's loved one. But, the even greater tragedy of the story was the fact that the injury and death did not come from a foreign enemy – it came from "friendly fire." This ironic term, "friendly fire," means that a courageous and dedicated service man or woman was actually killed or wounded by our own military forces. It was not intentional or planned. It was an accident or some kind of big mistake – but the result was just as disastrous as if it were a highly planned military action. It was "friendly fire."

Now, how does such a disastrous event have even a slight relationship to a Rotary club? Could you ever dream that loyal, dedicated Rotarians could take some very innocent actions, or inactions, or make mistakes that would actually harm or destroy their Rotary club?

The truth is, everyday I see the "friendly fire" of Rotarians giving blows, which are seriously injuring or destroying Rotary clubs around our country.

I first saw the "friendly fire of Rotary" coming from those Rotarians who insist that to be a good Rotarian you *must have 100% attendance*. These dedicated Rotarians could never believe that their 100% expectations or demands would actually be the deterrent to prospective new members, or could be the cause of current members leaving Rotary. Sure, many members take pride in their records of high attendance, and I commend them for their efforts. But, Rotary only requires 50% attendance. I have heard prospective members say, "Oh, I could never make a commitment for 100% attendance, or attending a meeting every week, so I couldn't consider joining your Rotary club." So, the "friendly fire" of those who preach 100% attendance, in their enthusiasm and commitment for Rotary, may actually be turning away excellent prospects or even causing the demise of good Rotarians.

Far too many of us overlook the impact that electronic communication has had on business and professional executives in recent decades. With I-pods, laptops, notebooks, I-phones, message texting and all the other daily new inventions, young executives are expected to be in constant communication to make momentary decisions in seconds and minutes. Corporate leadership may be thousands of miles away, but the instantaneous demands of business are found on their I-pod or laptop 24 hours a day. I know young executives who have been erased from their Rotary club membership lists, because their professional demands cannot always wait until 'after lunch.' If we want *new generations* to be Rotarians, I am convinced that some of us in the *old generations* must give a little slack, to the extent authorized by our by-laws.

The next "friendly fire of Rotary" comes from those devoted Rotarians who love their club meetings, pay their dues, enjoy the activities, take part in every service project– but sadly have never proposed a single person to join their club. These members enjoy all the benefits of Rotary, but have never given that same pleasure to friends or associates. Someone shared Rotary with them, but they have not taken the same step to invite other leaders of the community to join Rotary. These Rotarians would never think of hurting their Rotary club, but by never proposing other members, they may be directing a blow to the very heart of Rotary. New members are the lifeblood of a Rotary club. Sadly, nearly 80% of our members have never proposed a new member. I can't imagine that they don't have any friends. But, tragically, they may actually be part of the 'friendly fire" which eventually strikes a mortal blow to their club.

A third kind of the "friendly fire" of Rotary comes from those members who insist that the support and projects of their club should be directed just to their own community. These Rotarians know that every community has so many unmet needs, and insist that their service funds should be spent locally. One certainly could never criticize a club for meeting local needs. But, unfortunately, some Rotarians never see the equal value in reaching across borders or oceans to meet humanitarian needs of the world. This form of "friendly fire" actually deprives the Rotarians from feeling the great satisfaction of knowing that they can, in some small ways, make the world a better place. Local Community Service is vital to every Rotary club. But, also assuring that their Rotary club is part of the international community is a fundamental element of Rotary International. A club which does not reach out into the world is missing so much, because their club never quite achieves the full value of Rotary membership, and their Rotary members are the losers.

Another casualty of Rotary "friendly fire" is those clubs, which never seek publicity or promote the public image of Rotary. These clubs may conduct outstanding youth and community service activities, but no one ever knows. Their light is so hidden under a basket, that promising and eligible members in the community have no idea what Rotary is and what the Rotary club does. How can anyone aspire to become a Rotarian, if they never hear about the service projects of Rotary?

For an organization to survive in this century, it is essential that a strong, viable public image is portrayed in the community. The Rotary wheel should stand for service to our youth, for building a better community, for serving the needs of the aged, the disabled, the poor and the unfortunate. That is the kind of organization that bright, busy and committed young people will want to join. If Rotarians do not hold high the banner of Rotary and proclaim our good work, we cannot expect that it will be done by others. When we fail to showcase the good work of Rotary, it soon becomes the "friendly fire" which erodes the image of Rotary, and wastes golden opportunities to attract new members and strengthen Rotary's image in the world.

Another form of "friendly fire" comes from those Rotarians who continually fail to support The Rotary Foundation. So many of the rewarding activities of Rotary are the result of our Foundation – the Matching Grants, Ambassadorial Scholarships, Group Study Exchanges, The Rotary Peace Centers, the Polio Plus program, 3-H Grants, and other educational and humanitarian activities. The Rotary Foundation can only operate when it receives the annual funds contributed to Rotary; and yet, we have Rotarians who never bother to make a voluntary contribution each year. These are the same devoted Rotarians who regularly contribute to their church, their college, youth groups, health agencies, environmental organizations, hospitals, museums, and hundreds of other wonderful causes. But, for some reason they overlook an annual contribution to The Rotary Foundation. Contributions to our Foundation demonstrate pride in Rotary, and express a commitment to humanitarian and educational activities. How many say, "I'm a Paul Harris Fellow, so I've done my job." There is a good reason to say, "Every Rotarian – Every Year."

Another subtle form of "friendly fire" which frequently scuttles a Rotary club comes from the members who comment on every new idea with the announcement, "We never did it that way before." And, before you know it, the club is still back in old ruts following the same path of mediocrity. Those members who continually oppose change or new ideas would never consider their negative criticism to be "friendly fire" which annihilates the forward movement and enthusiasm of their club. Resistance to new ideas discourages membership growth and club retention, and can certainly be a deterrent to a fresh and dynamic Rotary club.

Of course, there are other ways that "friendly fire" may be suppressing the growth and future of Rotary clubs. Consider those who quickly dismiss a prospective member with the remark, "I don't think he is old enough to belong to Rotary;" or others who comment, "That business certainly isn't important enough to belong to our Rotary club." Occasionally you hear the declaration, "Our town isn't big enough for a second Rotary club," or, "We don't really have any women members, so I'm sure she wouldn't be interested in joining our club." In some clubs you hear, "They are the past presidents of the club, so we don't call on those guys anymore; they are kind of out to pasture."

Even you can hear in some clubs the saddest comment from the one who says, "I was really expecting to get involved – but nobody has asked me to take on a job or serve on a committee."

Such negative comments are certainly destructive forms of "friendly fire" which perpetuate the image that Rotary is not really a modern and vital organization in our community looking for eligible young members.

There is still another form of "friendly fire" which it is so hard to imagine that it could actually be a disservice to your Rotary club, because it is so unintentional. In many clubs there are those great Rotary friends who enjoy so much their long-time friendship week after week that they always sit at the same table. These Rotarians never realize that they are actually reducing the opportunities for friendship with other members of the club. I've been to clubs where someone will warn, "You can't sit there, that's Charlie's chair." There is nothing wrong with great friendships – but some times friends become so comfortable that it separates a small group from the rest of the members.

The tragedy is that these devoted Rotarians are unwittingly eroding the possibility of sharing their friendship with new Rotarians, prospective members or visitors. It is a tribute to Rotary that such wonderful, long standing friendships can be built in a Rotary club – but it is sad to realize that they may actually be causing other members to feel left out of Rotary fellowship.

We must remember that closed circles of friends can be a fatal form of "friendly fire" when new members or other Rotarians do not find the kind of welcome or fellowship they had expected from all club members – who thought that all members were going to be their new friends, and would welcome them into the club.

Have you ever wondered if there are members of your club creating casualties from "friendly fire?" Maybe it's only by accident, or thoughtlessness, or some mistake. Perhaps just some inadvertent comments or missed opportunities are delivering the blows, which prevent the club from moving forward.

The amazing thing about "friendly fire" is that nobody really intended to hurt their friends or harm the club they enjoy so much. It just happens because most of us have never stopped to consider what really builds clubs, strengthen clubs, and encourages prospective members. They could never imagine that their "friendly fire" could actually be harming their own Rotary club.

My message is simply this: The slow decline in Rotary's membership in some parts of the world, and especially in North America, is not the result of external enemies. Nobody has a campaign against Rotary. The media is not attacking Rotary. We have no public antagonists. The tragedy is that Rotary's casualties and loss of membership may actually be the result of "friendly fire" from of our own dedicated, but unthinking Rotarians.

My plea is simply for each Rotarian to pause and take an inventory of your own club. A Rotary club is too important for Rotarians to be shooting ourselves in the foot or even in our heart.

Remember these are the trademarks of "Friendly Fire."

- When the pressure for seeking 100% attendance turns away prospective members.

- When there are Rotarians who have never proposed a new member.

- If a club becomes so totally consumed with local projects that members never feel the real satisfaction of a grateful community on the other side of the world.

- When the name "Rotary" exists in almost complete obscurity in your community.

- When some club members are so reluctant to change, that they object to every new idea proposed by current leaders.

- When your club becomes so elite that members are putting artificial requirements for membership or provide no flexibility in understanding the demands on young and active executives and professionals.

- When a few members become so satisfied with their special friendships that they never think of expanding their circle of friends to visitors or new members.

- If any of these things are happening in your club, then we, too, may become the unwitting victim of that tragic calamity – the "friendly fire" of Rotary

The good news is that your club doesn't have to be the victim of "friendly fire." Decide today – I will invite a friend to join my club. I will sit with an entirely different group at next week's meeting. Decide today – that attendance is important, but it is not the only thing about Rotary. Decide today – let's make our club meetings even more attractive to leaders in our town. Decide today – we must try to understand the new professional and business demands upon our younger members, before we summarily remove them from our club rosters.

Each of us can build a better Rotary club. And if we can – we must. The Rotary club idea is far too great for any of us to let it fall into the arsenal of "friendly fire."

And if each of us does our part, we will never hear that knock on our door announcing the death of our Rotary club. We will not have to hear those words: "It was not by enemy action, the club was sadly destroyed by Friendly Fire."

Think about it – each of us has the answer. The future of your Rotary club and Rotary in the world is in our hands.

ROTARY'S INVOLVEMENT
IN POLIO ERADICATION

[The program to eradicate polio, called Polio Plus, has been Rotary International's primary effort for over 20 years. This speech was given to several Rotary clubs who asked if I would relate how Rotary International actually became involved in such a worldwide humanitarian effort.]

Rotary's Polio Plus program has been described as the finest humanitarian project by a non-governmental organization the world has ever known. Rotary has been nominated for the Nobel Peace Prize for our efforts. It is Rotary's project of the highest interest for over 20 years.

Many Rotarians have no idea of how Rotary ever became involved in eradicating polio in the world. So, let me recall the story.

In the 1950s, 60s, and 70s, virtually every person knew someone in their family or circle of friends who had polio. In the early 1950s, there were annually over 55,000 cases of polio in the United States. Worldwide there were perhaps 500,000 cases of polio. Of that number 50,000 children a year would die from polio and thousands more would be crippled, paralyzed or suffer lifelong disabilities.

So that was the backdrop of our story. In 1978, Rotary had a committee, appointed by R.I. President Clem Renouf, to design a new direction for Rotary. It was called the Health, Hunger and Humanity Committee. This was a small committee to design a program for Rotary International to undertake projects far greater than any club or district could do. Rotary had never undertaken a corporate or worldwide project – just club programs. I happened to be co-chairman of that 3-H Committee. We knew that if we didn't have an immediate success, the Rotary world would probably scrap the program the next year. So we looked for an "immediate success" project. We had about 16 projects proposed from around the world. One proposal was from the Philippines. Dr. Benny Santos wrote that if Rotary could provide the vaccine, they would mobilize all the Rotarians in the entire Philippines and immunize all the children. So, that was it. We approved the project; and if I recall correctly, some 6 million children were immunized against polio. It was a huge success. Pharmaceutical companies had other types of vaccine – for measles, tetanus, chicken pox and other vaccines, which were donated for Rotarians to distribute in several areas of the world. Rotary proved that immunization was the kind of project Rotary volunteers could handle.

A couple years passed, and another Rotary committee was created in 1982 by R.I. President Stan McCaffrey called the New Horizons Committee. This group had the job of "looking into the future of Rotary to see what tasks or new directions Rotary could take on the future."

I happened to be chairman of this committee. We considered hundreds of ideas – some big ones and some rather frivolous. Finally, I suggested that we ought to be thinking 20 or 30 years into the future. Why not do something big for Rotary's 100th anniversary coming up in 2005? A letter from Rotarian John Sever suggested that we consider providing polio vaccine for all the children in the world. The committee thought that was a good idea, so it was one of the 35 suggestions to the R.I. Board of Directors. So, in 1982 the Board of Rotary International approved the idea of giving polio vaccine to all the children in the world. The project was called "Polio 2005."

Two or three years went by, and finally in 1985, Dr. Carlos Canseco, RI Pres. from Monterrey, Mexico said that if we were going to get the task done by 2005, we should get started. So, he called Dr. Albert Sabin to Evanston and we had a meeting of some of the world's most distinguished medical and public health leaders. Dr. Sabin said it would cost at least $100 million dollars and we would have to immunize 500 million children. Wow what a job!

So, Rotary set a goal of $ 120,000 to raise the funds, and the name of the project was changed to "Polio Plus." It was the first major fund raising campaign by Rotarians of the world for a single project. However, by 1987 we had surpassed the goal and actually raised $240 million. So, Rotary leaders went to the World Health Organization and said we want to eradicate polio. It was not well accepted by all the WHO leaders who represented some of the most knowledgeable health authorities in the world. Rotary was "just a service club." Finally, when Rotary told them that we had over a million volunteers and $247 million in our pocket, they said, "Come on in." So we became full partners of the World Health Organization, UNICEF, and the US Centers for Disease Control.

At that time, in 1988, you could find polio in 125 nations of the world and it was estimated that there were 350,000 cases of polio in the world every year. But we took on the project – one country at a time. Our first big immunization day was in Mexico, where we immunized 13 million children. Then we went to Central America and South America. One nation after another became "polio free."

Rotary Clubs became "Polio Plus Partners" to raise funds for National Immunization Days. The Partners purchased iceboxes, colorful vests, caps, leaflets, street banners and many other items needed to mobilize whole nations to immunize their children.

Mary Elena and I were in India to participate in the national day of immunization. There were banners on the streets, parades, notices, distribution of thousands of radio and television announcements, plus handbills and leaflets. In that one-day over 125 million children received the two drops of polio vaccine. We have gone to some of the most poverty stricken areas of the Philippines, Ethiopia, Turkey and other nations to assist in National Immunization Days.

The project is an amazing and complicated one. Rotarians and health workers have to go to the most remote areas of the world by canoe, camels, elephants, horseback, motorbikes, and every other conceivable vehicle to reach all the world's children.

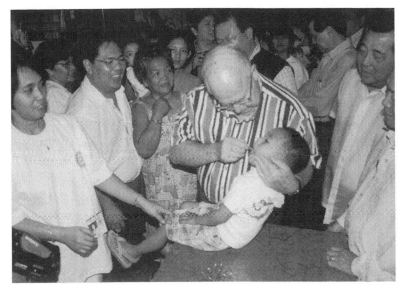

Rotarians volunteer for National Days of Immunization

I remember sitting on a rock on the side of a dusty road in Argentina giving vaccine to children in a remote area. Dozens of volunteer Rotarians, youth exchange students, health workers, youth organizations and other would go door to door urging parents to bring their children to get the vaccine.

Even in China, Laos, Vietnam, Cuba, Myanmar and other areas where there is no Rotary, we worked freely to distribute the vaccine. An interesting experience occurred in China. There was reluctance by China officials to accept vaccine from the Western Nations. We said, "Use Chinese made vaccine." But there was no polio vaccine made in China. So, Rotary said, "We will build a pharmaceutical plant in China, and made a grant of $18 million dollars to construct a factory in China. As soon as the project was under way, Chinese officials said now we will take the vaccine from the West. Immediately, China said all the children of China will be immunized, and in the first two days, 100 million Chinese youngsters received the polio vaccine.

The amazing thing is that the pharmaceutical plant in China has never produced one dose of polio vaccine, and the Chinese officials went ahead and immunized their children when they saw that Rotary International was serious about this mission.

We were not able to meet the target of a polio-free world by 2005, but we are close. Over 99% of the children of the world have received polio vaccine. You can find polio only in 4 nations, not the 125 countries when we started. We hope that we can soon stop the incidents of polio in Nigeria, India, Pakistan and Afghanistan. Last year there were only about a thousand cases in the world – compared to the 350,000 cases a year when Rotary undertook this humanitarian mission.

There are so many aspects to the polio story. I recall one day, when I was Chairman of The Rotary Foundation. We had a call from the World Health Organization, saying that they had arranged for a four-day cease-fire in the civil war in the Sudan so we could go in and immunize their children. But the WHO did not have any money to purchase the vaccine. I said, "How much does it take?" It was going to cost $400,000. I said, "You can have it immediately from The Rotary Foundation." The Chairman can make a grant up to $500,000 for an emergency humanitarian effort. The war stopped, health workers went in and immunized 3 or 4 million children – then the war started again. The World Health Organization said, "Of all the places in the world, there was no place we could turn – except Rotary, to make that project happen." Clearly, without the efforts of Rotary the achievements to eradicate polio would never have happened.

Perhaps some of you have participated in a National Immunization Day. It is an amazing experience. I remember when Mary Elena and I sloshed through the mud streets of a poverty stricken village in Ethiopia – one of the poorest nations of the world. The homes were nothing but shacks, dirt floors, which turned into mud with the occasional showers. Families cooked on wood fires outside their huts. This was the first polio immunization in this poor nation. In those few days, nearly 10 million children were given the drops of polio vaccine.

But of all the experiences of that day, I recall the ceremony to start the immunization. The President of Ethiopia was on hand. There were about a hundred little children lined up to receive the vaccine from their national president. And just at that time, on the other side of the room were about 35 small children, perhaps 5 to 10 years of age, all in wheelchairs, or leg braces, or crutches – they were all polio victims with bent backs and withered arms and twisted legs. They stood up the best they could and sang a song to the President. The song said: "It's too late for us – but don't let other children get polio. Do what you can to Kick Polio Out of Africa."

If you had been there to hear that song, "It's too late for us, but don't let other children get polio," you would know why Rotary has taken on this monumental task.

If we had only had the vaccine 2, 5, 10 years before in Ethiopia these children would be walking, running and playing, as children want to do. There are over

2 billion children who have received Rotary's polio vaccine – and they are now living a life without the fear of paralysis and death from polio.

We are on the verge of eradicating this dreaded disease. Perhaps next year, or the year after. And the amazing thing is it has been made possible because Rotary clubs, like yours, took a huge step some 20 years ago. Even today, funding is necessary. You may have heard that the Bill and Melinda Gates Foundation has contributed $350 million dollars to our efforts in recent months because they believe that Rotary will achieve this dream. Rotarians are matching $200 million dollars of the Gates gift.

That's the story of Rotary's involvement in our greatest humanitarian program – Polio Plus. And I thank every one of you who have been a part of this program for so many years.

The leaders of the world have clearly expressed that without Rotary International this monumental achievement would never be accomplished. We will eradicate polio in the world – and it will happen only because Rotary made a commitment some 25 years ago. And the world has learned that Rotarians keep their promises.

A ROTARY THANKSGIVING MESSAGE

[This address was presented at a traditional annual Thanksgiving joint meeting of five Rotary clubs in Stockton, California in November, 2006. A similar message has been given to Rotary clubs on other occasions.]

In this Thanksgiving season, Rotarians often pause in our hectic pace of living just to give thanks for some special things in our life. Years ago when I taught graduate students, I used to ask, "What is really important to you in life? Is there anything so important that you would give up your life for it?"

That would often start a lively conversation. What is important to you? Is it your children, your wife or husband, your country, your religion, your freedom, your house, your car, your golf cart, your remote control? You see we have so many things to be thankful for – such as living in this great state, in this part of a great nation, in this wonderful part of the world. We are blessed with riches beyond our capacity to count or measure.

The amazing thing is that we eventually find that the greatest rewards of life come not from attaining huge and momentous achievements or riches – but rather, from some simple words and acts of kindness, love, and caring.

I don't know of anyone who uttered from his deathbed, "Oh, I wish I had spent more time at the office, or had put more money in the bank." No, the last words are generally for the love and gratitude of family, friends and the affection of others.

Here is a story I read some time ago – perhaps over the internet. There was a man in New York City who loved to collect rare works of art. He and his son had a fantastic collection – from Picasso to Raphael. They would often sit together and admire the great art displayed in their New York mansion home.

When the Vietnam conflict broke out, the son went into the army and was soon sent overseas. He was a very courageous young man, but was tragically killed in the line of battle while rescuing another soldier in his unit. The father was notified and grieved deeply for his only son.

The following year, just before Christmas, there was a knock on his door. There stood another young man with a large package in his hands. The young man said, "Sir, you do not know me, but I am the soldier for whom your son gave his life. He saved several other buddies that day, and he personally carried me to safety when a bullet struck him in the heart and he died instantly."

He went on, "Your son often talked about you, and your great love for fine art." Then he held out the package. "I know that this isn't much. And I'm not really a great artist, but I think your son would have wanted you to have this."

The father opened the package. It was a portrait of his son, painted by the young man at his door. He stared in awe at the way the painting had captured the personality of his son. Tears welled in his eyes as he thanked the young man and offered to pay him for the portrait. The young man said, "Oh, no sir, I could never accept payment for what your son did for me. This is a small gift in his memory."

The father hung the son's portrait over his mantle. Every time friends and visitors came to his home, he took them to see the portrait of his son before he showed them any of the other great art works he had collected.

The years passed and the extremely wealthy man died. As his will directed, a great art auction was to be held for all of his collected paintings. Many influential art dealers and wealthy people gathered to see and participate in the auction of the magnificent art collection. There was great anticipation on who would purchase each masterpiece.

As they started the auction, the auctioneer unveiled the first painting sitting on the platform – it was the picture of the young son who had been killed in Vietnam. The auctioneer pounded his gavel: "We will start the bidding with this picture of the son. Who will bid for this picture?"

There was silence. A voice in the back of the room called out, "We want to see the famous paintings. Skip that one. And get on with the auction!"

But the auctioneer persisted, "Will someone bid for this painting? Who will start the bidding? Do I hear $200? Will someone bid $100?"

Another voice shouted, "Hey, we didn't come here to see this picture. We came to see the Van Goghs, and the Rembrandts. Come on – get on with the real masterpieces."

But the auctioneer continued. "What do I hear bid for the picture of the son? Who wants to take it?"

Finally, a small voice was heard from the back of the room. It was the longtime gardener who worked around the mansion of the wealthy man and his son. "I'll give $10 for the picture of the son."

The auctioneer continued, "I have $10 – now, do I hear $20?" Someone in the back of the room yelled, "Give it to him, and let's get on with the great art pieces."

The auctioneer called: "Going once, going twice – sold for $10." And he pounded the gavel on the table. A man in the second row shouted, "Let's get on with the sale of real art!"

The auctioneer laid down the gavel, and announced, "I'm sorry, but the auction is over." The crowd booed and yelled, "What about the other famous paintings?"

Then the auctioneer explained. "When I was called to conduct this auction, I was told of a secret stipulation in the will of this great art collector. I was not allowed to reveal that stipulation until this time. Only the painting of the son would be auctioned. Whoever bought the painting of the son, would inherit the entire estate, including all the other works of art. The man who bought the son's picture gets everything."

Why do I tell this story on this Thanksgiving eve? The message is that even small, seemingly inconsequential acts of service and kindness can be great treasures.

I have seen so many Rotarians who are waiting for the really big project to come along – then they will get involved. Some of us seem to be expecting that Rotary service has to be monumental or some highly publicized extravaganza before it merits our time, effort or support.

But the real work of Rotary is often the commonplace acts of kindness, and thoughtful service to others.

I recall some words of that great woman, Helen Keller, who said: "I always dreamed of performing some great and noble achievement. But, I am destined to perform just small and humble tasks, as if they *were* great and noble."

How can we give thanks for all the blessings, which have been set before us? I can tell you that right here in your own community there are many small tasks that can become great and noble.

There is so much to be done.

There are trees to plant; lonely people to visit; homeless who need shelter; food banks to be restocked; health clinics which need volunteers; meals to be delivered to shut-ins; clothing to be collected for the needy; books to be read to youngsters; museums which need aides; trash to be collected; graffiti to be erased; language to be taught; and old friends to be called. Oh, the list goes on and on.

You see, the greatest way Rotarians can give thanks for the great privileges we enjoy, is to look about the community and meet the critical needs of children, the disabled, the aged, the hungry, the homeless, the hopeless and those who just need a random act of kindness. There is service in the mere act of caring.

Someday, when you may be feeling down, stressed out, and merely holding on to your rope – consider this story. One day when Dr. Karl Menninger, the famous psychiatrist was giving a lecture on mental and physical health, a member of the audience asked: "Dr. Menninger, if a person was not feeling well, stressed out and thought a mental breakdown was coming on – what would you recommend?"

To everyone's astonishment, Dr. Menninger replied, "Lock up your house, go across the railroad tracks, find someone in need, and do something to help that person." You see, performing random acts of kindness and service is good medicine, too.

As I have traveled the world, I have watched Rotarians give their greatest gift, – their time, effort and concern – just to meet the needs of those who live in poverty, sickness, loneliness and without hope. These are not always monumental or world shaking events – they are just random acts of kindness, caring and thoughtful service.

I have frequently heard people say, "Sure, I'd like to do something worthwhile for others, but I just don't have free time." I usually answer, "Volunteer service isn't done just by people with time on their hands, – and it's done by people with caring in their hearts. Service can become a part of your life – not an add-on when you have extra time. We work, watch television, do the shopping, do laundry, sleep, eat, care for children, clean the house, go to movies, go to church, go to a ball game, play golf – we find time for everything. Why not put just 10 minutes a day to help others?

Just show a little love and concern. Do an act of kindness that no one expected. Give a hug. Make a compliment. Make someone's day. There really is someone who needs your pat on the back, or listening ear. There is somebody who needs you to care.

Oh, if there is any message I have on this Thanksgiving observance, it is simply this: Never forget that you are a Rotarian and Rotary is a *service* club. We meet and eat, have fun and enjoy the fellowship of others. But all of these enjoyable aspects of Rotary lead to our primary purpose – to serve our community and reach out to others around the world.

On this Thanksgiving eve, there is still time to demonstrate our gratitude for living in this splendid city, in this great nation and the pride we have in belonging to this amazing organization of Rotary International. Visit a friend, call a distant family member, stop in and see a neighbor, visit a rest home or hospital.

There is still time. It is not too late to give a check to St. Mary's Dining Room; the Salvation Army; the Children's Home; the Food Bank; a rescue mission; or some other group that will be feeding hundreds of hungry families on Thanksgiving. It is just one way to give thanks for the many blessings bestowed on each of us.

You may not know or ever see those who will be touched by your kindness. But this I do know, your Thanksgiving Day will be so much greater than you have ever known.

These may be just little acts of kindness, but to someone else, they may be giant moments to realize that someone cares.

Don't wait until the auctioneer starts to sell the art masterpieces – put your bid on the common portrait, which portrays the feeling of kindness and love.

That's when you can say: "I think we had a real Rotary Thanksgiving."

God bless you, and make this a very Happy Thanksgiving Day – not only in *your* home, but also throughout your *whole* community.

Happy Thanksgiving!

ROTARY'S ORIGINAL IDEA – VOCATIONAL SERVICE

[This address was prepared in 2003 for a Presidential Celebration on Vocational Service held in Vancouver, Canada organized by R.I. President Jonathan Majiyagbe. Subsequently, it was presented to many Rotary Clubs and distributed on a DVD]

No matter how much we like to think that Paul Harris and his friends created Rotary for such noble ideas of humanitarian service, goodwill and world understanding – it just was not the case. Rotary was started for business reasons and professional purposes. Paul Harris had the unusual idea that friendship and business might mix and result in even more business!

A century ago, Chicago and most large cities were in the grips of growing business and industry – both rife with fierce competition. Such slogans as 'Cutthroat Competition,' 'Let the Buyer Beware,' 'Dog Eat Dog,' and 'The Public Be Damned,' were commonplace in the lives of the giants of industry. Many business competitors were enemies. There were very few governmental restraints on enterprise, business practices or labor conditions. Business ethics, customer service, or professional standards were seldom topics for public discussion. Just making money was the goal of business and the professions.

It was in this atmosphere that Paul Harris, a young Chicago attorney, began to wonder if one person from each business and profession could actually work together, in a non-competitive situation, and help each other improve their business and income. If they were not rivals or competitors, maybe they could be friends and help each other achieve success. Thus, the idea of friendship and business was combined – and the idea of a Rotary club evolved.

As a matter of fact, the first constitution of the Rotary Club of Chicago, written in 1906, stated only two objects of the club. The first was: "The promotion of the business interests of its members." The second object was: "The concept of personal friendship." Although the wording changed slightly from time to time as the Object of Rotary was rewritten in subsequent years, the vocational service, or business element, was always retained.

I found an interesting comment, made by T.A. Warren, a British Rotarian, printed in a 1935 book on the early history of Rotary in Great Britain. Rotarian Warren became R.I. President in 1945-46. His observation was, "The only unique feature of Rotary is vocational service; everything else that we do is repeated by some other organization." In all of our earliest days, Vocational Service was clearly the primary focus of Rotary.

There were actually two separate directions of this unique business emphasis of early Rotarians.

The first was – "Rotarians Helping Each Other."

The members of Rotary were expected to patronize each other's businesses and recommend their fellow Rotarians to do business with their friends and relatives. At the early Rotary meetings, a common practice was for each member to report on which Rotarians he patronized during the past week, or had recommended to others. The early club had an officer called the *statistician*, whose duty was to compile each week all the orders that had been given or purchases received by members.

One story I heard many years ago from an early member of the Oakland #3 Rotary Club involved a member who was a haberdasher or clothing storeowner. During the meeting, he slipped out into the hallway where the members had hung their hats. He checked the labels in each hat. He stormed back into the club meeting and announced that; "Some of you Rotarians have purchased your hats from my competitor. That's not the Rotary way! So, I quit this club!" And he did. He truly was a *mad hatter.* But, that was the concept – Rotarians helping each other in their business and professional pursuits, and expecting others to do the same.

The early history of the San Francisco Rotary Club tells of the emphasis on promoting business at club meetings. As you know, San Francisco was Rotary's second club. It was the custom that prizes were frequently awarded at club meetings to the member who had made the most purchases from other members during the previous month. H.J. Bru Brunnier, a charter member of the San Francisco Rotary Club reported that he won the prize one month by buying 72 separate items from Rotarians to furnish his new engineering office in downtown San Francisco. Incidentally, Bru Brunnier became president of Rotary International in 1952-53.

It was also recorded that in the meeting room of the Rotary Club of San Francisco in the early days, a series of shelves were installed for members to display merchandise. Ten minutes of each meeting were devoted to members giving short talks about the quality of their own goods and services – in other words – a Rotary commercial.

On some occasions, clubs used the "Rotating Five Dollar Bill." This would be a five-dollar bill, with a slip of paper attached, on which a Rotarian would sign an endorsement when he purchased an item from another Rotarian. He in turn would use the bill to purchase an item from a fellow member, and around it went. At the next club luncheon, the five-dollar bill, with all the endorsements, would be exhibited as an example of the practical application of the concept that Rotary promoted good business.

San Francisco members were also urged to send advertising literature to each other's homes in order that their wives would know where to make purchases from Rotarians.

It has been said that this same concept of promoting business led to the first community service project by the original Chicago Rotary Club. In promoting more business, the members decided that since the women did most of the shopping in downtown Chicago, they would do more shopping if they didn't go home so quickly. What was the answer? If there were public toilets in downtown Chicago – the women shoppers would stay downtown longer. And this is what they did – installed the first public restrooms in downtown Chicago. When service is provided – business is enhanced. It was on that basis that the world's service club movement was launched.

The second major direction of the early Rotarians was: "Promote Higher Ethical Standards in Business and Professional Practices."

It was said that in the early meetings of Rotary, the members frequently discussed techniques to improve their business practices and offered wise and friendly counsel to each other. If a Rotarian's advertising seemed misleading, if members heard negative comments about the quality of another member's products, or if there were steps a member could take to greet his customers in an improved manner – those and many other business topics might be fair discussion at a weekly club meeting.

Soon, the members and their friends began to feel that when you do business with a Rotarian, you would always be treated properly, that a Rotarian's word could be counted upon, and that there was a high ethical element in all transactions. Thus, the word, *Rotarian,* was considered a real mark of distinction in the business and professional world – perhaps comparable to the word, *sterling*, found on a piece of quality silverware.

The Chicago Rotary Club, and others which followed, created a *Committee on Business Methods*, which concentrated their attention to the business practices and the public confidence of each enterprise represented in their community. The Rotary clubs were regarded as the leaders in fighting corruption and unfair business practices. In 1910, Rotarian Arthur Sheldon, spoke at Rotary's first Convention in Chicago, saying, "As man comes to see that right conduct toward others pays; that business is the science of human service, and that *he profits most who serves his fellows best."* Thus, this basic principle of business ethics became Rotary's first motto: "He Profits Most Who Serves Best."

In passing, it might be noted that just a year later at the 1911 Convention in Portland, Oregon, Ben Collins, the president of the Minneapolis Rotary Club told that his club used the principle of *Service Above Self* in all their business and professional activities. And Rotary's second motto was initiated. Both of these mottoes were officially adopted many years later at the 1950 Convention in Detroit.

As Rotary continued to expand around the nation, it was not uncommon for Rotarians in the same profession to meet and discuss business ethics and fair dealings in business practices. They frequently discussed standards by which business and professional practices should be judged. After several years of preparation and debate, in 1915 Rotary was ready to adopt a *Rotary Code of Business Ethics* when they met at the annual convention in San Francisco.

The *Rotary Code of Ethics* was not a law or rule, but rather it was an expression of determination for Rotarians to maintain certain basic ethical and honest standards in one's business or profession. The code could only be enforced by example, friendly influence, and encouragement; however, it set a very high standard for men who were Rotarians.

As years went by and Rotary became more of an international organization, *The Rotary Code of Business Ethics* became more difficult to translate and use as a working document in changing worldwide business and professional life. In 1978, the Code was withdrawn from circulation and the 1980 Council on Legislation approved an amendment to the R.I. By-laws to delete any reference to *The Rotary Code of Business Ethics* in all future literature and publications of Rotary International. So, that is why many Rotarians have never heard of this document, which had such a significant impact upon the early development of Vocational Service.

I first heard the phrase, *The Rotary Code of Ethics,* when I was a very new Rotarian. About a dozen new members of the Berkeley Rotary Club were invited to an informational meeting, hosted by Les Hink, the owner of Hink's Department Store, and probably the community's most influential citizen. It was an honor to be in the home of this distinguished Rotarian.

Before the evening ended, Les Hink told a story, which I have remembered for over 45 years. He said, "When a group of my friends were trying to charter a Rotary Club in Berkeley in 1916, I told them I really wasn't interested in some luncheon club. But, one day, a friend brought a copy of *Rotary's Code of Ethics* to my office, which I read, then read again. I thought if this is the kind of organization, which believes in honesty, fair play, high ethical standards and decency in business practices – then I want to belong to such a group. He joined the Berkeley Rotary Club. As he concluded the evening, Les personally presented each one of us a parchment scroll, rolled as a diploma and tied with a ribbon. It was *The Rotary Code of Business Ethics.* When he joined Rotary in 1916, it was the most important reason for him to become a Rotarian and he thought it would have the same meaning to each of us.

In the years following World War I, dozens of trade, manufacturing and professional associations developed and adopted codes of business standards and fair practice. Automobile dealers, sales organizations, restaurants, travel agents, and many other professional associations drafted new standards of business methods, which recognized that each had an opportunity to serve society and at the same time eliminate the sharp and shady practices, which had been so customary in many industries. Many of these occupational improvements were led by Rotarians who frequently met at Rotary Conventions in vocational groups to discuss improved business methods and standards.

In 1943, another significant step was taken when the Rotary Board of Directors adopted a 24-word statement on business practices – originally written by Rotarian Herbert J. Taylor of Chicago. That statement, which has become known as the *Four Way Test*, has become a guide for sales, promotion, advertising and many other relationships with dealers, customers and employees. The simple philosophy of the 4-Way Test was created by Herbert Taylor in 1934 during the Great Depression, when Taylor was called upon to take charge of the Chicago-based Club Aluminum Company, which was facing imminent bankruptcy. He created the test as a measure of the company's fairness, honesty and integrity in all of their business transactions. It became the personal standard of the employees in making all business decisions.

The Four Way Test. "Of the things we think, say or do: 1. Is it the truth? 2. Is it fair to all concerned? 3. Will it build goodwill and better friendships? 4. Will it be beneficial to all concerned?"

This Four Way Test is not a code, creed, or pledge, but rather four questions for self-examination and improvement in one's dealings with others. It is a simple and practical guide for all human relationships. The Test has been printed on thousands of articles, plaques, billboards, and posted in schoolrooms and public buildings, and been the topic of hundreds of essay and speech contests.

In the 1960s another concept was introduced to Rotary clubs to promote Vocational Service – the Case Study of principles and new methods for handling situations. This technique, which had long been used in universities and business schools, became a valuable practice to promote vocational service and share business experiences in Rotary club meetings, conferences and assemblies. The discussion cases would present business dilemmas, which had serious ethical problems for managers, or conflicting interests among employees, stockholders, customers, and suppliers. In most of the cases studied, there were usually no 'right answers,' but rather they provided the opportunity for Rotarians to explore moral, business and ethical dilemmas.

Vocational Service gradually emerged into a wide variety of other Rotary activities. Rotary clubs sponsored vocational guidance experiences for young people, such as job interviewing training, vocational guidance camps, vocational schools, Camp Enterprise, Junior Achievement and career information sections in public and school libraries. Other Rotary clubs have initiated special vocational programs for disabled persons to prepare them for useful occupations.

In 1965, The Rotary Foundation established one of Rotary's most popular and rewarding programs, which combined vocational service and international under-standing – The Group Study Exchange program. Since that time, over 35,000 young business and profession-al men and women have participated in GSE teams of four or five persons in international travel, combined with vocational observations in other nations.

By the 1980s, Rotarians once again directed their at-tention to business and professional relations by urging Rotarians to maintain a balance between the natural desire for success in one's vocation and the neces-sity to maintain ethical, honest and *dignified* business practices. Finally, in 1989, the Council on Legislation adopted a new statement, called a *Declaration For Rotarians For Business and Professions.* This eight-paragraph declaration provides a more specific expla-nation or guidelines for what the phase *'high ethical standards'* actually means in the Object of Rotary.

The *Declaration For Rotarians in Business and Profes-sions* once again reiterates that a Rotarian's vocation is considered "to be an opportunity to serve society" and an obligation to improve the quality of life of one's community and the dignity and respect to all useful vo-cations. The Declaration continues to emphasize the importance of honesty, high ethical standards and fair-ness to employees, associates, competitors, custom-ers and the public.

Today, it seems as if society has come full circle in the question of business ethics. Large corporate execu-tives, accounting firms, stock brokerages, governmen-tal officials and other business managers are under indictment and investigation for unethical and illegal practices. Huge segments of the population have lost saving and retirement funds because of shady and shameless corporate dealings. Much of the confidence in business and professional trust has been eroded and lost. Some areas of business and government have been described as *morally and ethically bankrupt.* Perhaps the time has come for Rotarians to restore The *Rotary Code of Business Ethics* and to take the lead in proclaiming business honesty, ethical dealings, truth and fairness in all relationships.

If Vocational Service was the basis for Rotary's activities in the beginning of our first century, this may be the time to revitalize business and professional ethical concerns as Rotary's primary responsibility. The time is *NOW* for Rotarians to redirect our attention to vocational service and the vital importance of ethics to the daily operations of every business and professional endeavor.

That was the meaning of Vocational Service a hundred years ago, and it is equally important and vital in the Rotary world today.

UNWRITTEN HISTORY OF ROTARY

(The very first humorous speech I made before a Rotary club, some 50 years ago, was a spoof on the history of Rotary International. This speech has been revised many times to fit different audiences. A few of the ideas came from a humorous book I read during my college years. This rendition is one which I delivered in 2009 at the breakfast meeting of Rotary International of Great Britain and Ireland at the R.I. Convention in Birmingham, England.]

On occasions like this it is becoming customary to call on some of the old Past Presidents of Rotary to talk about how things used to be. Old Past RI Presidents and Past District Governors have a tendency to come to these events and just sit and drool. But these long serving Rotarians are really wonderful folks and we love them – kind of like an old pair of tennis shoes, all worn out, except the tongue.

Today I am going to talk a little bit about the history of Rotary. I know what is going through your mind – that has to be the dullest topic in the world. No, I have some speeches which are even duller.

I met a friend on the street the other day who said to me, "If you think you know so much, why don't you write a book about Rotary's history." Well, I just chuckled and pushed him in front of a passing car. But, it occurred to me afterwards, maybe that was a good idea – so, I decided to look into the history of Rotary.

It was particularly interesting to find that the history of Rotary goes all the way back to the beginnings of the club. This fact, which I discovered rather early in my research, saved a great deal of time.

So, when did Rotary really start? The earliest account of Rotary dates back to ancient Greece in the year 500 BC – when a luncheon club was formed by three fellows named – Aeschylus, Sophocles and Euripides – Rotarians never used their last names.

Rotary didn't start out as a luncheon club... it really was a supper club... with a very early cocktail hour.

In Greece, all the best people knew a good thing when they saw it. All the wealthy men of Athens belonged to Rotary. Why, their District Conference was always held at the Parthenon.... it was the highlight of the social season. They would dance to the best band in the land – Oedipus Rex... Fling and Flex with Oedipus Rex was his motto.

It was in Athens that the Rotary symbol was developed by a fellow named Nick. He had been struck in the head by a passing chariot on the way to the Rotary luncheon – at the Athens Motel Six. When he arrived he had kind of a "run down look." Actually the imprint of the chariot wheel had been left on his forehead. Well, the good natured, fun loving Rotarians quickly adopted a wheel symbol – to preserve the memory of 'ol Nick.

The second Rotary club was formed in Rome. The annual kick-out meeting or changing of officers of the Rome Club was always considered the best meeting of the year. They held it at the Coliseum. They say it was a touching sight to watch the lions rush at the past president.

The stunts of the Birthday Committee provided the Rome Club with some special fun. One occasion, during the presidency of Julius Caesar.... all the Rotarians just called him Julie, a guy named Brutus, the Sergeant-at-Arms, entered the room with a large birthday cake. It was generously covered with dozens of flaming candles. That wasn't unusual – since even then, the average age of a Rotarian was 84.

In the excitement of singing "happy birthday dear Rotarians" the cake tipped over and the candles ignited several togas. The flames spread to the Rotary club banners hanging on the wall. As the room was engulfed in flames, President Julie, who was always a precise fellow, saw it was time for the luncheon program.

Fortuitously, they had arranged for a musical program... a young violinist, named Nero. In spite of the flaming walls of the Rome Hilton... young Nero proceeded to fiddle until exactly l:30 sharp. Well, as you can imagine, the whole town was burned up about this... and the Rotary club was forced to flee to the West.

We next found Rotary developing in France. Napoleon was a Rotarian. For a number of years, Napoleon belonged to the Waterloo Club.... He held the classification of Past Service.

France is where we saw the first woman in Rotary. It didn't start out that way. There was this fellow named, Jack of Arc – who was a cross dresser. When the Rotarians found out that Jack was really a young woman, named Joan, they took swift action. They ceremoniously removed her from the club – during the club's annual barbecue.

Legend tells us that Christopher Columbus was also a Rotarian. He was the inter-city chairman of the Venice Club. One day, Ol' Chris took a boat trip to the West and missed four meetings in a row without a make-up. And poor Chris was automatically dismissed from Rotary.

Moses was a Rotarian, too. He was the guy who created the 4-Way Test. He took those tablets and went up into the hills. When he came back he had l0 commandments. The Rotarians could never remember the l0 Way Test – so he just cut it down to 4.

Most of you know when Rotary started in Great Britain and how you got that RIBI thing. The early Rotarians developed a slogan – "Rotary Is Better In England." As the years passed, they just assumed that everybody knew that Rotary Is Better In England. That's how they got the acronym, RIBIE. So, finally they just dropped the last word, England, since everyone knew that. And we now have RIBI. That's the way it all happened.

And all the Districts in RIBI used to have a great fair, which was held annually in Coventry. There was competition among all the districts for the best parade entry. The District Governors always judged the parade entries. But would you believe that every year at the Coventry fair, the District Governors picked as the best entry, the "horse and rider entry" sponsored by the Inter Wheel Club of Coventry.

History shows that Rotary soon had a good start in Ireland. It was about this time that the people were fighting the Boer War... and the Rotary club had some of the biggest bores in the country.

And I hear you ask – Who brought Rotary to the United States? The Pilgrim Fathers, no less. They had all been members of the Rotary Club of London... until the club president... a fellow named Big Ben, classification of watchmaker... oppressed the members with such cruel and inhuman fines they decided to start a club in the New World. So the Pilgrim Fathers sneaked a copy of the Manual of Procedure and set out across the Atlantic – after getting a good price on a Hertz rent-a-boat.

Rotary has always been proud of its record of high attendance. Stories are told about one of our early members – a fellow called Paul Revere, classification – lantern lighter. History shows how Paul Revere rode furiously from village to town... but the truth is he wasn't concerned about the Revolutionary War... he was just trying to attend 12 make-up meetings in one day.

George Washington was also a Rotarian of great distinction. There was an old saying about George...first in war... first in peace and first to be an early leaver. He was the Club Service chairman of the Mt. Vernon Club. George was chairman of the Tea Party at the Rotary district conference in Boston. For fund raising he planned the dollar-throwing tournament across the Potomac.

George had this friend who made up that first Rotary flag – Betsy Ross. It really was Betsy who always had a lot of fabric scraps cutting lying around, so she started that little club banner idea for visiting Rotarians. She gave the idea to Russell-Hampton.

Really, all the finest men of the colonies were Rotarians...Ben Franklin, the only fellow with the classification of kite-flying – wholesale; and John Hancock, the club secretary; and John Marshall, Sergeant-at-Arms... Dan Webster, a guy you could always count on to give a speech if the program didn't show up... yes, all the leaders were Rotarians...well, all except one – Benedict Arnold – he was a Kiwanian.

Well, Rotary flourished for several decades... until an incident at the District Conference – the one held at Fort Sumter. There was a misunderstanding with a few of the clubs from matched districts...Robert E. Lee and Ulysses Grant – they were district governors at the time... mixed it up during the fellowship hour. Well, the dispute lasted for four years. It did, however, provide the basis of some pretty spirited inter-city meetings. Finally, the controversy was settled the year the RI Convention was held at Gettysburg. The RI President, a fellow named Abe, classification of rail splitter – retail, gave a short speech and brought Rotary back together again.

But then Rotary expanded.... and as it expanded, it grew larger. I think all of us thrill at the sound of the names of some of our great leaders of our organization.

There was this fellow who had the boat building classification – a guy named Noah. He was the guy who changed the classification system. Noah felt that there should be two in every classification. It was Noah who started that whole thing.

And then they brought women into Rotary – and they added so much. There was Elizabeth Taylor – classification of "housekeeper" – she was divorced 8 times and kept the house every time. And Estee Lauder – she had the idea of Rotary make-up. Scarlett O'Hara – she started that idea of serving Southern Fried Chicken at Rotary lunches. Judge Judy – Sergeant at Arms. And Monica Lewinsky – she was head of the Fellowship Committee – ah… I don't remember her classification.

I remember a couple other very active members – Robin Hood and Jesse James. They were fundraisers for the Rotary Foundation. You might recall the Jesse James Fellows.

One of the fascinating things about Rotary has been our annual President's themes. We have had great themes for centuries. It's funny how some themes seem to catch on. Even today, I see around town some of our great Presidential themes – Stay Off The Grass – Watch For Falling Rocks. And probably the most popular presidential theme of all time was – Have A Nice Day, or maybe Honk If You Love Paul Harris.

Well, maybe that is enough of Rotary history. I think I had better save the rest of my notes for the question period, which will be held at the bar shortly after we adjourn.

The whole point of this irreverent and absurd history of Rotary is that Rotarians must have fun. The work of Rotary is serious – but Rotarians don't have to be.

Friendship is strengthened when Rotarians laugh and enjoy some time together.

Rotarians may never recall exactly what a speaker said or what a club program was about. But, they always remember how they felt. If they had fun, or were inspired, or motivated – they will always remember how they felt going to their Rotary club meeting.

All of our programs of service depend upon good friends who enjoy the fellowship of Rotary. Our club meetings have to be fun. Laughter is *great medicine*, even for a Rotary Club. The enjoyment we find in Rotary is the beginning of service. When we have a job to be done in our community, we don't look around for strangers to do it – we start with our friends – our Rotary friends.

When Rotary took on the task of eradicating polio in the world – that was serious business! We have immunized over 2 billion children against polio – that is over 99% of all the children in the world. When we set this goal, over 20 years ago, there were as many as 500,000 thousand cases of polio in the world each year. Until last year when there were less than 1000 cases of polio in the entire world. And this serious work will not be finished until we complete immunization in the last few countries. And we will reach this goal this year or next.

When we are feeding hungry people – that's serious business. When we are building low cost shelters, or providing clean water, or building clinics or libraries – that's serious business. It is serious business when we restore sight to the blind, and lift a disabled person into a Rotary purchased wheelchair. It is serious business to restore a school, or equip a hospital in a poverty area of the world. Those are things which our Rotary Foundation is doing every day.

Let's never forget what Rotary's real business is. We are not just in the business of meeting and eating. We are in the business of *fellowship and service.* Let's enjoy the great fellowship and friendships we have in Rotary, just as we are rewarded by the satisfaction of service projects well done.

Every day, every hour and every moment, somewhere a Rotarian is extending a hand of friendship and service.

The activities of The Rotary Foundation are like a pebble dropped into a lake, and the ripples go on and on. You never know where the ripples of your personal efforts will go or who they will touch.

So, enjoy Rotary. Have fun, laugh, tell stories, make new friends and serve until you find happiness all your life.

And by the way, did I tell you the story about the two Rotarians and the farmer's daughter who had car trouble on a country road...

Oops, I think my time is up! So, I'll save that story until another day.

THINKING OF OUR FUTURE

[This short speech was prepared in 1993 for the Rotary International Convention in Melbourne, Australia when I was serving as President of Rotary International. The purpose was to urge Rotarians to look at our changing society and to accept the fact that the organization must also change.]

The Rotary International President spends a great amount of time in airplanes. Flying 37,000 feet above the surface of the earth, you have a lot of time to think. So, perhaps it is not so unusual that the Rotary President thinks about Rotary today and what we will become in the future. Are we doing enough to keep the Rotary spirit alive in the world and can it survive in the future? That is also one of the benefits of Rotary conventions or conferences. We can get away from our daily tasks and have some moments to think about the fellowship and future of Rotary.

I often wonder how long Rotary International will survive as a world organization. The life expectancy of mankind today is about 80 years, plus or minus. So, Rotary might be considered to be in 'the critical years.'

Some time ago I read an article by an Austrian psychiatrist named Frankel, who was held in a Nazi concentration camp during World War II. He told stories of his fascination with the thoughts of his fellow inmates. He said he could divide them into two groups. The first group were those who concentrated on their past. They would constantly recall the good times and the good meals they used to have. They lived with thoughts of their earlier days.

The second group, according to Frankel, were those who talked mostly of their future. They would continually dream of their future. They would discuss the good meals and good times they would have as soon as they were liberated from their prison existence.

Following the war, Frankel learned that very few of the first group, those preoccupied with the past, actually survived their horrible ordeal. But the surprising thing was that the survival rate of the second group, those concerned with the future, was much higher. Looking to the future seemed to be a reason for survival.

Occasionally, I have thought about that story, and wonder how many Rotarians are looking backwards rather than to the future? Are too many Rotarians living in the past; holding fast to the Rotary that used to be; instead of concerning themselves about the Rotary of the 1990's or into the 21st Century? At this great convention, I hope we can capture a new vision of the reality of Rotary today and dream a bit about the potential of our future.

How much are we preparing for the future of our organization? What is the character of your Rotary club?

Are your members more concerned about preserving its past, rather than planning for its future?

How about your club's membership? Are you making the adjustments that a changing society requires? The stagnant growth pattern of Rotary throughout the world appears to be an early warning system. It is an alert call for all clubs to take a look at what Rotary is doing and how Rotary is perceived in your community.

At the early part of the 20th Century, the Baldwin Locomotive Works was one of the most profitable companies in the United States. It was clearly the nation's largest producer of steam locomotives. It was a national industrial leader – but it went bankrupt for one simple reason. It didn't plan for what was happening in the marketplace.

You see, the company thought they were in the business of *building steam locomotives.* But the truth was, they were in the business of *transportation!* They failed to plan and adjust to the changing forms of transportation and the changing marketplace of the world.

How often do we forget what a Rotary club's main business is? We are not in the business of just meeting and eating or holding on to ageless traditions of our weekly meetings. Our business is fellowship and service to our community and the world. If we forget this – we do so at our own peril.

Any organization, whether it is a steam locomotive industry, or the most international service club in the world, has to understand its role in the world. Then we must anticipate the future and prepare to make forceful, courageous and imaginative plans. Once the vision is determined, there must be a willingness and dedication to translate those plans into action. In my opinion, Rotary's vision and destiny must be to place *service to others* as our number one objective. But, even with *service* as our objective, we must never forget that service must begin with the *fellowship* we find in our weekly club meetings.

As I have visited the Rotary clubs of the world, I frequently wonder if we are preparing for the realities of the changing business and professional communities of the 21st Century, or are we preparing to perish because we are not making the adjustments the marketplace will demand. None of us should be afraid of change – but rather embrace it for its positive values.

If Rotary International is to exist in the 21st Century, we must be prepared to ask some probing questions:

• What are we doing to make Rotary attractive to young business and professional leaders in our community?

• What will happen to those clubs more concerned with attendance records than service activities?

• What is the future of those clubs, which find it so much easier to write checks to other community groups, than to put their own hands to work in a community service project?

• What will happen to those clubs which spend more time protecting timeworn territories than demonstrating active willingness to spread the good work of Rotary by creating new kinds of clubs and memberships?

- What will happen to those clubs which fail to realize that some of the most qualified and highly trained business and professional executives in their community are women?

- What will happen to those clubs which seldom see beyond their community borders and overlook the amazing international service potential of our organization?

- What are we doing that is relevant to the critical issues in our communities – drug and substance abuse, homelessness, AIDS epidemics, deteriorating family life, illiteracy, polluted air and water resources, the erosion of business ethics and moral deterioration, and dozens of other issues which are chipping away at our society?

As much as Rotarians may enjoy the pleasant weekly gatherings and fellowship we find in our clubs, we must not overlook that Rotary must be on the cutting edge of societal issues if we are to be relevant to our community and potential members.

If Rotary International in the 21st Century is to survive and escape the tyranny of mediocrity, it will take Rotarians of vision, with the energy and enthusiasm to experiment, explore, build, innovate, and unlock new resources.

As you listen to the programs of this convention, let yourself dream a little – but don't go to sleep! Ask yourself: How am I building my club? How is my club preparing for the future? How can my club become a high priority in the life of young, busy, mobile executives – in the same way that it has been in my life? Is my club living in the past – or are we preparing for a new century?

If you continue to ask yourself these questions, I am certain this convention will be one of the most meaningful ever held.

I conclude with these final comments, which actually relates to the Rotary theme for this year. Some days I think:

- *There isn't much that I can do* – but I can share Rotary with a friend.

- *There isn't much that I can do* – but I can volunteer to help on our community service project.

- *There isn't much that I can do* – but I can help someone by sharing some flowers, or sit a few minutes with a sick friend, or give a book, or call a person who I know is lonely.

- *There isn't much that I can do* – but I could invite a Rotary Youth Exchange student or Rotary Ambassadorial Scholar to my home for dinner.

- *There isn't much that I can do* – but I will be glad to greet visitors at our club meetings with a warm and sincere welcome.

- *There isn't much that I can* do – but I could contribute to the Rotary Foundation, even though my gift might not be as large as other people may give.

- *There isn't much that I can do* – but I could collect food for the hungry, or seek shelter for the homeless, or reach out to ease a pain or lift a burden.

- *There isn't much that I can do* – but I could plant a tree, or tend a garden, or volunteer at a local school or youth group.

- *There isn't much that I can do* – but strangely enough, whatever I can do always seems to bring wonderful joy and satisfaction into my life.

Maybe that truly is the meaning of our theme – Real Happiness Is Helping Others.

And if I could dream just a bit, I'd say, that message may be as relevant in the 21st Century as it is today. At least it is worth considering. So, if you are around in the next Century, why not give it a thought?

SCOUTING AND ROTARY

[Because of my long involvement with the Boy Scouts of America, I have frequently spoken to Rotary clubs about the historic relationship between the Boy Scouts and Rotary. This is a speech which has been used on several of those occasions.]

February is an important month in the history of two distinguished organizations in the United States. On February 8th 1910, the Boy Scouts of America became a chartered organization in New York, and then spread across the United States.

Likewise, on February 23, 1905 the first meeting of a group which was to become Rotary International was held in Chicago. These two international organizations, which had their origin in the early days of the 20th Century, have had a long, close and historic relationship. So, let's review how Rotary and the Boy Scouts of America have been intertwined for nearly a century.

The Boy Scouts of America grew out of a youth group, which was organized in England in 1907 by Lord Robert Baden-Powell to provide effective training in character building, good citizenship and personal fitness for youth. Scouting soon became a program for boys to enjoy participating in outdoor activities, to develop peer group leadership opportunities, to create good friendship, and to explore various careers, hobbies and special interests.

Since that early beginning in England, International Scouting activities have grown to be the largest voluntary youth movement in the world, with a membership of more than 25 million members.

The world Scouting program has expanded to over 155 nations and territories. Just like Rotary International, World Scouting has effectively overcome barriers of language, customs, race and religion.

Rotary and Scouting has had a long time relationship

In the United States, the Boy Scouts serve nearly three million youth each year, and involve well over a million adult volunteer leaders in 53,000 community troops, packs and Explorer teams. Each local Scout troop has traditionally been sponsored by a chartering organization, such as business or labor groups, churches, schools, service clubs, PTAs, and veterans groups. At one time, Rotary clubs in the United States chartered and sponsored more Boy Scout troops than any other organization. Although many Rotary clubs still sponsor local Scout troops, churches have taken the lead as the number one chartering group. And this is rather predictable, since many Rotary clubs have moved into Interact and RYLA as their major youth activities.

From its earliest days, all Rotary clubs were encouraged to have 'Boy's Work' as a standing committee in each club. It was recognized at that time that boys comprised the vast majority of juvenile delinquents, truants, and law violators, and often had very few role models to guide their lives. Rotarians saw the opportunity to act as mentors to youth groups to guide them into proper routes of community citizenship. So, the Boy Scout program became a natural avenue for Rotary club sponsorship.

The primary reason that Boy Scouts and Rotary have had such a close relationship is that many of the fundamental characteristics of both organizations are the same. Just as Rotary's codes of ethics, The Four Way Test, and high standards of personal values and friendships are basic goals to all Rotary clubs, the Boy Scout movement is based upon similar principles of service to others, truth and honesty, respect and tolerance for one's religious beliefs, duty to country, responsible citizenship, and high personal and moral standards.

The very essence of the Scout Law, which each boy learns and repeats, is common to the values of a good

Rotarian. A Scout is: trustworthy, loyal, helpful, friendly, courteous, kind, obedient, cheerful, thrifty, brave, clean, and reverent. Those are the features, which also identify a good Rotarian. U.S. President George W. Bush made an interesting statement a short time ago, when he said: "The goodness of a person and of the society in which he or she lives often comes down to very simple things and words we find in the Scout Law. Every society depends on trust and loyalty, on courtesy and kindness, on bravery and reverence. These are the values of Scouting, and these are the values of Americans."

Fundamental to the Boy Scout promise or oath, are the words *To Help Other People At All Times.* There is hardly a better description for a Rotarian or a Rotary club. The Rotary motto of Service Above Self certainly captures the same principle of helping others at all times.

In any review of the major service projects of Scouts and Rotarians over the years, you will see so many similarities. Both organizations have been active in drug abuse prevention programs, collecting food, helping with war refugees, promoting safe driving and bicycle safety, highway and community clean-up campaigns, protecting the environment, rehabilitation of those with disabilities, blood drives, recycling, disaster relief, and many other activities to build better communities and promote good citizenship.

And the Boy Scout motto – *'Do A Good Turn Daily'* – describes the admonition we often give to new Rotarians. So many times, I have asked Rotarians to merely do just one act of random kindness each day and their lives will reach a new level of satisfaction in their business, family or community relations. Can you imagine the impact on our communities if a million Rotarians and a million Boy Scouts were each doing some unexpected act of kindness or a Good Turn each and every day for someone – without any expectation of personal return? That's what Rotary's motto of *Service Above Self* is all about. So, you see there really are some interesting similarities between the two organizations.

Another similarity is our worldwide extension. As I mentioned a moment ago, the World Scouting movement has been organized in 155 nations of the world, just as Rotary clubs are found in 180 countries. As I traveled the world, I frequently met Boy Scouts, and was actually made an honorary Scout in several nations. In Sweden, I recall discussing the Boy Scout program with the King of Sweden, who is actively involved in promoting the scout principles among the youth of Sweden. He was most interested in Rotary's support of the Boy Scout movement.

I recall one very hot day in Nigeria, when a ceremony was held to make me an honorary Boy Scout of Nigeria. There were about fifty boys in their colorful uniforms escorting me to a huge bonfire. In Scouting, boys love to sit around a large campfire to tell stories or sing songs. But this was in the middle of the day, with 115-degree temperature in the heart of Nigeria, and they had a 40-foot high campfire to emphasize the important nature of the ceremony for their foreign guest – the President of Rotary International. I was presented with the official neckerchief and made an honorary Boy Scout of Nigeria. And I was impressed.

Around the world I met many Rotarians who are volunteer leaders of Boy and Girl Scout troops. In the world of Rotary we have many groups, which we call 'Fellow-ships of Rotarians' with common hobbies or special interests. One such group is the International Fellowship of Scouting Rotarians. At every Rotary International Convention, the International Fellowship of Scouting Rotarians meets to explore new ideas to support youth programs in their communities.

As you now know, the International Fellowship of Scouting Rotarians, in cooperation with the Boy Scouts of America, have created a special award for Rotarians who have given long and dedicated service to the Boy or Girl Scout Movement. This award, with its attractive certificate and medallion, is called *The Cliff Dochterman Award* to honor individual Rotarians who serve as role models and render distinguished and dedicated service to the Scout movement in their community and nation. I have to admit that I am always honored, and humbled to present 'The Cliff Dochterman Community Organization Award' of the Boy Scouts of America to a fellow Rotarian.

I confess that I'm always a little embarrassed to present a certificate with my own picture on it. A couple years ago, when I was walking down the hallway at the Rotary International Convention in Salt Lake City, a Rotarian came past me and looked at my name badge. He said, "Are you Cliff Dochterman?" I assured him that I was. Then he responded, "Well, I have The Cliff Dochterman Award from the Boy Scouts. I thought you must have been dead years ago!"

For many years, Rotary International presented the 'Rotary Award for World Understanding and Peace' to a non-Rotarian or organization for outstanding achievements consistent with the ideals and objectives of

Rotary. This was Rotary's highest award for international service. It is interesting to note that in 1984, the Rotary Award for World Understanding and Peace was presented to the World Organization of the Scout Movement at the RI convention in Birmingham, England. Clearly, Rotary has always respected the great work of Scouting in the world.

Perhaps many of you were Boy Scouts in your younger years, or have served as volunteer adult leaders. Over the years, I have observed the great satisfaction, which a man has when he says, "I am an Eagle Scout." The Eagle Scout award is the highest achievement a Boy Scout can earn. Only about 5% of the boys who enter the Scout program have ever achieved that level of recognition. In the nearly 100 years of Scouting in America, almost 2 million boys have worn the Eagle badge, out of the 110 million boys who have started up the achievement ladder.

In a recent article, I read that between 30 and 35% of all the Air Force and West Point cadets were enrolled as Scouts, and over 14% of those young men were Eagle Scouts. And of the 312 United States astronauts, 180 were involved in Scouting, and 40 were Eagle Scouts. So, it is easy to draw a conclusion, that the training of the Boy Scouts of America really is effective in preparing young men for quality citizenship. And the same can be said for the Girl Scout programs.

For nearly a century, the Boy Scouts of America and Rotary International have grown together and made a great impact upon our nation. I think that this was especially well said by the late U.S. President Gerald Ford, who was an Eagle Scout, and a long time supporter of the Scouting movement. He spoke at a major

Scouting meeting in Washington D.C. during his presidency, and made this comment:

> *"If the goals of the Scout Oath and the Scout Law are not the goals of the people of the United States, and what they want their President to live up to, then I must draw the conclusion either you have the wrong man, or I have the wrong country – and I don't believe either is so."* He went on to say, *"I happen to believe that the ideals and aspirations of all Americans and all Scouts are one and the same. And I will continue to use those ideals as a guide and as a compass in all my official duties."*

I suggest that the ideals of the Boy Scouts and Rotary International are those, which provide a worthwhile direction and clear-cut mission for all of us. That is why, I am proud to be both a Rotarian and an Eagle Scout.

Rotary and Scouting truly have shared a common interest and a great influence on the youth of our nation for nearly a century. I commend all of you who give your time, effort, and personal resources to care for and serve the youth of your community in Boy and Girl Scouting, the 4-H Clubs, Boys & Girls Club, YMCA, in youth athletic teams and in other ways as good and positive role models.

I trust that for many years to come – Rotary and Scouting will continue to work together to train young people in good citizenship and high standards in all they do. Those are the boys and girls we hope will be our future Rotarians.

It is a great legacy for two outstanding organizations.

CONVERSATIONS WITH PAUL HARRIS

[This humorous presentation was originally prepared one afternoon in a hotel room at the Rotary International Institute in Anaheim about 2005, when I was asked if I would make an address at a dinner meeting that evening, because they had no speaker. Since that time, I have revised and expanded the speech several times to fit specific audiences. This rendition was given at the 100th Anniversary of the Los Angeles #5 Rotary Club in January, 2009.]

How many times have we repeated the story about that historic meeting on February 23, 1905, when Paul Harris met with three friends, Hiram Shorey, Silvester Shiele and Gus Loehr, to explain his idea of a new businessman's club in Chicago? Did you ever wonder what happened the next day, when Hiram Shorey got to thinking about the idea and called Paul Harris at his office? The day was February 24, 1905.

Hirum wore a cap and had little round glasses. The phone rang in Paul's office and the conversation probably went something like this.

"Paul, Hiram here, I've... ah... been thinking about that idea of the club you suggested last night... Where did you get that idea? Oh... You're what... a kind of ... a ...lonely guy, Huh? You don't have too many friends... Well, most lawyers don't. Paul... have you thought about getting a dog? ... A dog is man's best friend...

Paul... I've been wondering about a couple of those details for that new club you were talking about.

Paul... it... ah... It wasn't quite clear to me why you call some of the meetings, 'conventions' and some 'conferences?' What? ....Oh, you will explain that... at... the what? At the Assembly. Or, maybe at a workshop? .... Well, frankly, Paul, I can't quite see the difference... What's that... there really isn't much difference... Don't you think his club has an awful lot of getting together?

What's that..."The More We Get Together, the Happier We'll Be"... Paul, are you singing? ... So, you want this club to meet *every* week, huh?

Unless we "make up"? Ah, what's a make up, Paul?... Oh, it's what... just another meeting... What's that? You make up either 2 weeks before or 2 weeks after... unless you are excused... That's a little confusing, if you ask me.

And what? You're going to keep attendance records each week... and give a ribbon at the end of the year... You mean just a little piece of cloth? Oh, boy, that... ah sounds like a *real* incentive, Paul. What?.... You think people will do just about anything to get a ribbon... Well, we do give ribbons at the county fair... but that's usually for the best hog...

The author has a "conversation" with founder Paul Harris

And what will we do at the meetings? Hear a speaker *every* week? ... Well, won't we run out of speakers...You think there are a lot of people who want to talk?... and what? Rotary will never pay for a speaker... Paul... what kind of speakers do you expect to get for free? ... Oh, they don't have to be good... just free.

What's that? You had another idea? ...You want to call my wife what?.... You want to call her, ANN. Where did you get that idea, Paul? No, No, her name is Hortense... You think all the ladies would like the name, Ann? Paul, you don't know my wife...

And another thing... What is this Rotary Foundation thing you keep mentioning? ... Oh, it's just a fund raising scheme, huh...All you want is the money, huh, Paul? You think guys will give you money just to be called a *'fellow'* huh? Wow, Paul...you are really full of...ah...full of ideas.

And ah, what are you going to do with the money? Oh, just spend it on *good things*...huh? That's what my wife says too, Paul. But, the money always seems to go... and she hasn't found *a thing* that isn't good *for her!*

And another thing... you mentioned something about a 'Youth Exchange,' are we expected to exchange our kids? ... I don't think my wife wants to give our kids away...Oh; it's just a *vacation exchange*. What...ah... what do we exchange them for? ... You mean we have to take somebody else's kids, huh? Man... that's a real bummer. Although we've got a couple kids I'd exchange for about anything.

And would you tell me once again... why do you want just one person from each business? .... Well, ya know Paul, ah...Noah had two of each...but you only want one...You think we aren't expecting any more big floods...you think what.... Someday we are going to have what...Global Warming... and another big flood? Paul... your ideas are getting pretty far out for me...

And you suggested another thing...you want to serve chicken at every Rotary meal... Why is that? ... You what? Oh...your brother-in-law owns a chicken farm...

Sure there are lots of ways to serve chicken... But *every* week?

And another thing, Paul...tell me about this singing at the club meetings? You think that...ah...singing adds just a little culture, Huh? ...You think, "I've Been Working On The Railroad" is a real culture song, huh?

And you thought of another song by just spelling RO-TARY. What's that? R-O-T-A-R-Y... is that supposed to be a song? Well... sure, Paul...it sounds a little catchy... but how many times can you spell Rotary in one song?

Now, did you say that one person would be called a ... what...a District Governor? And trained at an International Assembly? What's an Assembly Paul? ... Oh, a 7 day meeting? Hum...You think it would take an entire week to train a district governor?... Sure, if you say so.... But, God did the whole world in 7 days... Well, I'd agree, God never tried to train a District Governor.

But, Paul, what if they picked a jerk for this governor guy?... You'd still send him to the training meeting... and what?... yeah, you would just end up with a trained jerk.

I was thinking about your RIBI scheme for some special organization in England and Ireland...Do you think that is really necessary?...You don't...but the British like it, huh? Yeah, the British like anything that is a little different... Yeah, you are right... but just not quite as different as the French...huh? Paul, you really are a funny guy!

Paul, that got me to wondering...do you really mean you are letting people into the club who don't speak English. ...But, how will they know what we are saying... You what? You just speak *louder*...and they will understand... well, I guess so.

Paul, another thing... How are the members supposed to know all of these rules? You'll write them in a big book called <u>The Manual Of Procedure.</u> How big is the book, Paul? You mean it will be 300 pages long? Couldn't you just make it a little simpler... maybe just a little booklet and call it <u>The ABCs of Rotary</u>?

And Paul, you said something about PETS...are we all supposed to get a dog or cat? We could teach them to do tricks....yeah, my wife has a canary which can whistle 'Dixie.' But some people are allergic to cats....

What? Oh it's not an animal... just another meeting... Presidents-Elect Training Seminar... Oh, a PETS training for club presidents... Sure... I get it, just teaching old dogs new tricks...

But, one other thing, Paul...will you tell me again what the club is supposed to do...Oh...just save the world... yeah, that's a big job... But... You'd keep it a secret? No Rotary advertising... Oh, so you save the world... but don't let anyone know... I tell ya, Paul, that's kinda strange...

And, what was that 4-Way Test thing you kept mentioning? ...You...ah.. just kept asking questions. Where are the answers? What? There aren't any answers... Then... why ask the questions? Oh, I see... it's just an idea to sell plaques, huh? And then ... you're going to start a company...you'll call it what? Russell Hampton?

And about this sport jacket thing... Do you really think all the guys would wear the same color jacket? Oh... it sure is a good idea... especially for the fellow who sells jackets.

I tell ya' Paul, this whole Rotary thing sounds pretty complicated to me... I'd better think it over a little longer... Frankly, I don't think your club idea is really going to swing...

But, I'll tell ya', how about this, Paul... if someday you'd just like to go out to lunch... Why don't you just give me a call? Well, so long, Paul, I'll be seeing you around."

Well, that may have been the conversation 100 years ago, but what about today? Fortunately for us, AT&T has some very new technology – it's called the *heavenly connection.*

Let's see what we can do... I have a cell phone here... "So, AT&T, connect us with heaven... I'll wait... No, I'm calling from Los Angeloc...no, no not Salt Lake City..."

They have nice music... I believe its harps... Oh, What a Friend We Have In... "Oh, yes ...No, that's not the number I wanted...it was PAUL HARRIS.... I didn't want to speak to Henry the Eighth....Well would you try Paul Harris' cell phone...?

Can you hear me now? ... Can you hear me now? Good, good.

Well, Paul, we've kept that ol' Rotary club going for a hundred years... It's what? ... Oh, it's a surprise to you, huh? Especially with some of the leaders we've had...

What's that? You can hardly wait to see next year's leaders?... Well, they *are* a motley gang. There are new club presidents and District Governors... and Assistant Governors, too. Yeah... there are a lot of them...What's that? ...You think a little more *quality* would be a lot better than all that *quantity*...I'll make a note of that.

But, tonight Paul I'm calling from the great Centennial Celebration of the Los Angeles Five Rotary Club... Oh it's a big party... Lots of folks here... All dressed up....

Yeah... Paul, they are still using your name, and your picture is on everything... By the way, Paul, did you ever have a picture taken when you were younger?... You didn't ...well OK, we're still using the old bald one... yeah....

And the club here in L.A. had a great Centennial Community project – called 'Rotary House'... it's a wonderful shelter and service center for homeless people... yeah, working with the Volunteers of America...

This "Rotary House" is for homeless people...Yeah, they just don't have a house...well, I don't know how they get their mail...maybe nobody writes to them... But it is sure a great Community Service project.

Sure, Paul... we all remember that you had a great Community Service project in Chicago... you built toilets in downtown Chicago... Oh, your project was a good one alright....but most of the towns now have public restrooms... No, Paul, a flush toilet is not too big of a deal today...

Let me tell you, that all the Rotarians here remember the many times you personally visited the LA 5 Rotary Club... I bet those visits were some of your *most favorite* memories... Oh... They weren't...huh.

Well, they still speak highly of you... and they recall Homer and Walton Wood and his friend Jerry Muma... they really got this club started back there in 1909... Sure, I bet they were all your good friends... too.

What's that? ... Oh, you really do remember the first R.I. Convention you had here in LA in 1922... And they had another one in 1962... and again in 2008... yeah, just a couple years ago... Oh, it was a great one....

This gang here in Los Angeles did a fantastic job hosting the Rotary world in 2008... Oh, everyone said it was one of Rotary's two greatest Conventions... Well, Paul... modesty prevents me from mentioning the other one.

And Paul... you will like this... Rotary got its name in the Guinness Book of records during the Convention... Well we recorded the largest collection of donated books... Yeah, a huge pile of books for school kids in Southern California... I knew you would be pleased...

What's that? You say that Rotary was in the Guinness Book once before... When was that? ... Paul Revere? Are you sure? You say Paul Revere was racing from village to town on the 18th of April of '75, and hardly a man is now alive who remembers he made 16 make-up meetings in a single day... I never heard that before.

Paul are you dreaming...Come on...Yeah, Rotary Makes Dreams Real.... But I find that Paul Revere thing hard to believe....

Oh, sure, Paul.... in 2005 we had a really great Rotary Centennial Convention... too. Yes, it was in Chicago.... Yeah, right in downtown Chicago... Yeah, we know you lived there... and you were a lonely guy... But it's hard to be lonely in Chicago today...

And we had a huge parade in Chicago... bands, and floats and motorcycles... All kinds of things in the parade... No, I don't think we had an elephant... except Republicans...That's funny Paul... Sure, I bet the parade was as big as the one they had for Capone....

Well, Paul, the men and women of Rotary have really done a great job...Yeah, Paul... women. You must have already heard that...since 1987... No, they don't take a back seat... Paul... They want to drive the bus!

I'll tell you Paul, we're also celebrating Rotary's achievements in the Polio Plus program...You're right... you haven't seen many kids there with polio lately... Yep, that's what Rotarians have been doing... Over 2 billion kids have received the polio vaccine...You're right, Paul...it's some kind of a Rotary miracle.

I tell ya', Paul.. we've had Rotary club 100-year celebrations that are really super... in San Francisco, and Oakland... and Seattle... and right here in Los Angeles...

And by the way, there is a whole book on the History of Rotary... yes, it starts at the beginning... No, Paul, you can't edit it... its already written.

Oh, there are a lot of good stories... No, Paul, historical books don't have to be true... Have you read Bill Clinton's book? Oh, it's what? His book is not in Heaven's Library... You'd have to go where to find it... Oh, down there... And all the copies have been checked out... by whom? Oh, the Kiwanians. .. Yeah, Paul, that's funny...

And another thing... This Los Angeles Club has an International Centennial Project, too... it was in Uganda... They are building latrines with running water for some schools... Yeah, Paul we still remember you built the toilets in downtown Chicago...

You are right, Paul... this LA5 Club has a history of great projects... You still remember them, huh? ... That was the Crippled Children Society back in the 1930s... And you recall how they supported the Settlement House project... Sure those were great community services...

And they started the DARE program to teach kids the dangers of drug abuse... and the Rotary High Five Project.

Sure, this Centennial event has given them a chance to look back on 100 years of great service... Ok, I'll tell them that you send you personal congratulations...

Well, Paul... this Centennial here in Los Angeles is about the biggest thing since... sliced bread... Yeah... Paul... the bread comes already sliced now... No, you don't cut your fingers quite so much...

Well, I think all the Rotarians are having a great Centennial... What's that? "A Centennial only happens every hundred years"… Paul that's a good line… You always were a funny guy…

Well, that's about it… So, I'll be saying, "Goodbye," What's your last word? "Just tell 'em you are there in spirit."… There you go again… Paul… I'm sure they will get the message.

So long, Paul… we're always thinking of you…"

By the way… Paul says, "Hi."

If there is any message in these conversations, it is simply this: You have to have fun in Rotary. The work we do is serious – but Rotarians don't have to be. In Rotary we can enjoy good friends, have a few laughs and enjoy the fun of being a Rotarian.

When we provide clean water, or educational equipment, food or medicine in poverty areas – that is serious business.

When we immunize 2 billion children and work to make the world polio free – that is serious business.

When you lift a child who has had polio or a birth defect into a Rotary donated wheelchair – that is serious business.

When a blind person is given back their sight at a Rotary eye clinic – that is serious business.

But when we sit around the tables of 33,000 Rotary clubs with some of our closest friends we can enjoy some of the finest fun and fellowship ever known.

So, each time the bell rings in your Rotary meeting, or you put on that Rotary pin, just remember how lucky you really are and what a proud distinction it is to say, "I'm A Rotarian."

And it all began because a hundred years ago, a group of businessmen believed that they really could build a better community and a better world through Rotary.

That truly was a Dream Made Real.

ROTARY'S MEMBERSHIP GROWTH

[This speech was given to the Rotary International Assembly in 2008 to the audience of incoming District Governors. Some of the comments have been used in other presentations, particularly seminars promoting membership growth and retention.]

If I said, "I have some beautiful flowers here in my hand," I am sure you would not believe me. You can easily see that all I have is a package of dried brown seeds. These seeds are not beautiful flowers, and they never will be unless we do something very important. We must plant them, water them, give plenty of sunlight and help them grow, if we want beautiful flowers to develop. In the same way, Rotary membership in your District will not grow or blossom, unless some very necessary steps are taken.

Why do Rotary International leaders keep emphasizing membership growth and development? The answer is easy – Rotary's very survival depends upon membership growth. It is a universal maxim; *an organization either grows or dies.* Just like a beautiful bouquet, we must replace the old flowers with new flowers, or the bouquet will soon wither and die. Tragically, other service clubs are suffering the disaster of declining membership. We must not let that happen to Rotary.

As you travel throughout your Districts, you will be asked, "How do we expand our club's membership?" So, let's talk about how you are going to help your clubs expand their membership?

There are three distinct ways for Rotary membership to grow:

Number 1 – You can seek new members for your club.

Number 2 – You can retain your current members in your club.

Number 3 – You can sponsor a new club in your community.

Let's look at some practical steps, which a club can take to make each of these three actions happen.

Number One. Rotary grows when you seek qualified new members. A club must have a specific plan. The plan can take various forms. But, the plan or the goal must be measurable. Just to say, "Our club needs more members," is not a goal at all. It must be specific. If you say, "We will bring in one new member each month," that is a real goal. It is measurable and accountable. So, how will you find that new member?

Your specific plan could be based on a 'team approach' with several members on each team. The team will meet and discuss qualified business, professional and community volunteer leaders who should be in Rotary. The team members will visit business establishments and talk with the managers and supervisors. They will also discover executives who may work from an office in their own home. They should seriously consider persons who may be the primary volunteer leaders in the community, even if they are not attached to a business or profession.

Another plan is to identify prospects by assigning two members to visit the establishments which are not represented in Rotary. Representatives should be invited to Rotary as guests to learn more about Rotary.

A third plan could be to establish one club meeting per month to be a *'visitor day'* to which all club members would invite a friend or prospect to enjoy the program and learn about the good work of Rotary in their community.

A fourth plan is designed around Rotary Foundation alumni. Seek out those who may have been an ambassadorial scholar, a member of a Group Study Exchange team or a former member of Rotaract. These are natural prospects and so many alumni report that no Rotarian has ever invited them to a Rotary meeting.

Another effective plan is when every club member is invited to prepare a list of their personal contacts – name their accountant, attorney, dentist, physician, minister, adult sons and daughters, business dealers or suppliers, insurance executive, and other individuals whose services they seek and use. From these lists, the membership team may create many prospects to be guests to the club, and frequently membership prospects develop.

One effective plan for those clubs which have a substantial number of retired Rotarians is to ask each retired person to name the best person in the community who is performing the work they previously did. New prospects may quickly develop.

Another plan is to look into your community for diversity. Are there ethnic communities where Rotary is not known or ever considered? Are there areas where Rotary has somehow neglected to seek membership?

Another promising plan is to extend a welcome invitation to women business and professional executives and eligible spouses of Rotarians who fulfill the requirements of membership. If you have clubs in your district, which still believe that men are the only business and professional managers and supervisors in the world, then you may also have an informational task to perform. Much of the business of the world is being conducted by outstanding women and they deserve to be in Rotary. If there are Rotary clubs, which can't handle this, then step out and organize a new club in your community, which includes both male and female members who fully meet the qualifications of Rotary.

I am sure that there are other effective plans to identify and invite deserving men and women into Rotary. It is well known that the reason many highly qualified managers and executives do not belong to Rotary is the simple fact that they have never been asked. Your task, as District Governor, is to give clubs practical tools to create a specific plan to identify the men and women who should be qualified *'prospects,'* and then to invite them to become active Rotarians.

Let's move to the second topic. We can expand Rotary membership by *retaining the members you currently have.* Every business knows that it is far easier to retain a good customer than it is to *find a new one*. We know that about 15% of all Rotarians leave Rotary each year. Obviously, we are unable to change the fact that each year some Rotarians will die. But, what suggestions are you going to give your clubs to retain their current members who drop out of their Rotary club? And many Rotarians leave within the first year or two after joining.

The first step to retaining a member occurs the day a member joins the club, or maybe even before. A high quality orientation about Rotary is absolutely vital. Each new member deserves a dignified introduction to Rotary. New members must be given information about the interesting history, traditions and customs of Rotary. Sponsors or senior mentors can introduce new Rotary experiences to new members. All new Rotarians must be brought into the wide circle of friends we call the Family of Rotary.

The second important step is immediately to give each new member a worthwhile and meaningful task within the club. The new members must be involved in the social and service activities of the club from the very outset. Only when a new member begins to feel that he or she has a useful job will they feel that they are fully a part of the club, and that they have actually become a Rotarian.

A third suggestion for retaining members is to recognize the impact modern technology is having upon young business and professional people today. The demands on the 21st Century executive or manager are far different from those of 30 or 40 years ago. With I-Pods, lap tops, text messaging, I-Phones, and the ever increasing technical forms of communication, the current executive is expected to be making instant decisions, and be on call 24 hours a day, even when offices may be located on the other side of the world. Many managers and supervisors do not have the option to make a decision or respond 'when I get back from my Rotary lunch.' I see far too many young Rotarians and even prospective members being pushed out the door when their clubs still insist that 'our standard is 100% attendance.' Our by-laws only expect 50% attendance. The truth is, if we want to attract new generations to join Rotary, many of us in the older generations must be willing to change some of our thinking, provide a little more freedom in our regulations, and give a lot more consideration to the demands and expectations which business and professional executives face today.

Another serious retention factor is the degree to which new members are actually welcomed into the old established circles of the club. How many clubs have that wonderful group of long time Rotary friends who always sit every week at the same table, and would never think of inviting a new member or prospect to join their group? Have you been to a club where they say, "Oh, you can't sit there, that is Charlie's chair – he has been sitting there for the past 20 years!" These wonderful friends would never think that they are actually depriving other members of their friendship and are not actually part of the total fellowship of the club. Soon, new members and visiting guests realize that they have not become a part of those small circles of friends. And someone who intended to be a good Rotarian becomes a casualty to Rotary.

One of the most critical reasons that we do not retain some members is the fact that the quality of our club meetings, service activities and social events are just not worth the time of busy people. Club meetings must be interesting, enjoyable, fun and worthwhile if we expect to retain the interest of business executives. A club which settles for dull, uninteresting and poorly organized meetings will be a club with real retention problems. Rotarians should look forward to attending an interesting weekly meeting, or they may soon find themselves passing by their Rotary meeting to accept other business, family and community responsibilities.

Another significant retention step is to assist a member to join another Rotary club even if they are leaving your club by changing business or moving to another town. When a good Rotarian moves away, we have a responsibility to advise the club in the other city that a Rotarian has moved into their community. We may lose a member in our club, but can retain him or her in Rotary by suggesting their name to another club.

Finally, we must be alert to the symptoms, which lead to resignation. Frequently missed attendance, failure to participate in social events, lack of interest in service projects or club fundraisers, apparent family or business problems; these may all be signals that a member may soon resign. Here is where club leaders can have a kind personal discussion and may save the prospective dropout. Just a telephone call to say, "We miss you," may be one step in retaining a member whose interest level is *on the fence*. Occasionally, a thoughtful conversation may provide an answer to a potential retention problem. That is the real spirit of the Family of Rotary.

Now, let's look to that third procedure to build Rotary membership – *you can sponsor a new club in your community.*

Of course you will hear a few of those well-worn comments: "Our city is too small for another Rotary club;" or, "We tried that once before;" or even, "If there were any qualified people, we would take them into our club."

Those are not the comments we need to build Rotary membership for the future. No one suggests building another Rotary club just like the one we have. Why not think about a *new* kind of Rotary club in your community?

How about a new Rotary club with all young executives and professionals under the age of 40? The nucleus of this new club might be former Rotaractors, former Group Study Exchange Team members or Foundation alumni, or even young executives whose schedules make it impossible to attend at the time the older clubs meet.

How about a new Rotary Club in an ethnic or minority section of your community and chartering a group who share common economic and cultural interests, but, may have never have been invited to the older club?

How about a new Rotary Club composed of both male and female executives in a community, which has not previously taken the step to include women members in Rotary?

How about organizing a new Rotary club for members who are unable to attend traditional luncheon or dinner meetings? This could be a breakfast club or late afternoon meeting club. Consider a club with sack luncheons and no fees. Maybe start a Saturday club which meets at a golf course an hour or so before tee time. There are younger generations who have the same motivation for service and fellowship, but they may also have entirely new concepts of how and when a Rotary club can meet and function.

How about a new Rotary club in a shopping mall or an airport complex? Or even consider a high-rise office building or on a large university campus. Don't think about cloning your existing clubs. The new century of Rotary requires and permits a new vision of fellowship and service.

Our original question was: How can we help Rotary membership to grow? Remember those brown dried flower seeds? We said they would only become flowers after they were planted, given sunlight, pulled out the weeds, and cultivated to grow. So, Rotary will only grow when you take some important actions. Your clubs must have a plan to find and invite new members. Your clubs must become so effective that they will retain their current members. And, then reach out into new segments of our communities and build new clubs.

If Rotary is to grow, we must take action. We must take action if you want beautiful flowers to bloom. (*Display a bouquet of flowers from under the lectern.*)

No longer can Rotary International permit a slow decline in our worldwide membership. Rotary *can* blossom – just like those dried brown seeds.

My friends, you are the leaders. The task is in your hands. Membership development is up to *you*. The bigger question – are each of *you* up to the task? I think you are – so go to it!

LIVING YOUR FAITH FROM MONDAY THROUGH SATURDAY

[Occasionally I have been invited to "fill-in" for a minister at a Sunday Church service. This address is one of the "sermons" I gave in 2008 which had special references to my Rotary experiences.]

A few years ago, I had the opportunity to be the world leader of Rotary International, the very first and most international service organization in the world. Perhaps you have seen the signs at the outskirts of most cities that "Rotary Meets Here" on Tuesday noon, or Wednesday morning. Perhaps your assumption is that it was just a meeting and eating organization.

The fact is that Rotary International is a service group in 33,000 communities in 200 nations and territories of the world. One million, two hundred thousand business and professional men and women formed a fellowship for the purpose of cultivating high ethical standards, building better communities, and conducting educational and humanitarian projects to improve the quality of life for all people.

As the world president of this international association, for a couple years I traveled to every part of the world, meeting with heads of state, promoting humanitarian projects in developing countries, and assisting volunteer community leaders to give their time and energy to serve others – without any thought of personal return.

You may wonder what that has to do with a message for this church service.

Let me illustrate with this personal experience. A short time ago, I was having dinner in Chicago with a group of Rotary International leaders. As we talked, I looked around the table. On my right was a gentleman from New Jersey of the Jewish faith; next was a Hindu from India; the third man was a Catholic from Brazil; then there was a Muslim from Egypt; the fifth gentleman was a Lutheran from Norway and finally one Methodist from California.

Here we were, six individuals, coming from six religious faiths; our primary languages were different; our nations were under different political structures; we represented different social customs, and even had differences in the way we dressed. But we were working together to meet human needs in a world filled with poverty, illness, illiteracy and hardship – and we were trying to build bridges of friendship and peace.

The interesting thing was that in each of those six religious faiths represented around that table, the basic tenets were the same. We were all taught by our religious faiths to have a concern for our brothers and sisters; we were all taught to care, to help, to lift, to share, to love and to live in peace. We just happened to be brought together through a worldwide organization that day. But, it was easy to recognize the universal truths, which were common in the spiritual experiences which guided each of us.

Obviously, Rotary is not a religion – but it provides a means by which people can put their religious faith into their daily life.

Have you ever thought about all of the many ways we actually express our religious faith? We attend church; we offer prayers; we support our Church with our time and gifts; we read the scriptures; we sing the songs; we may continually study the words of God; and there are many other forms of religious traditions.

And being a life long Methodist, and attending so many church dinners, I think Methodists must also find some type of spiritual meaning in a potluck supper.

But perhaps the most difficult thing is to put our faith into daily practice in our lives from Monday to Saturday. How do we "live" our faith from Monday through Saturday?

My question is how do we *practice* what we *hear preached*?

Have you ever responded to a real call for help? It might have been a call from your own children, a neighbor in need, a community group, your associates in your business or profession, or even from someone in desperate need some place in the world. Do you know what it is like when some one really needs you? Remember that song of the sixties – "People Who Need People – Are the Luckiest People in the World."

And then, after you responded to that call for help – can you remember how you felt? Can you recall the pleasant feeling, the happiness, the real joy or even the quiet satisfaction with which you were filled – because you helped someone who needed you?

One of the observations I have made in my lifetime is that the search for individual joy, satisfaction and happiness is a universal dream. Among the happiest people in the world are those who discover the great satisfaction and enduring rewards, which come from the simple act of serving and helping others. Perhaps you have recognized that the men and women who achieve real happiness – which is the deepest of human longings – are those who have found a cause or need so compelling that they are willing to give a major portion of their lives to fulfill that purpose.

I have always been intrigued by a statement made by the late Dr. Albert Schweitzer, the dedicated physician and African missionary. While talking with a group one day he said: "I do not know what your destiny will be – but this I do know – the only ones who will find true happiness in life, are those who have searched and found how to serve others."

As I traveled the world, I have observed the miracles of men and women helping others. I have seen the tears of joy, which our volunteers experience when they remove the bandages from a blind person who has been given cataract surgery – and a formerly blind person sees his grandchildren for the very first time. What an experience! I observed the smiles of excitement as a pump brings fresh clean water from a newly sunk village well, where women had formerly carried water for miles every day. I remember one occasion when we dedicated a new water pump in an African village. In the middle of a village of grass houses, the new water pump became the center of community activity. For generations the women had carried water twice a day for over a mile from a polluted stream. Now the simple water pump gave them clean water right in their village. The women gathered around washed their clothes, sang songs, and the children ran around and played. As we were dedicating the pump, a woman was saying something to me. I asked my interpreter, what she was telling me. He said, "She is telling you that when the volunteers gave them the new pump – their children stopped dying."

I have heard the laughter of excitement as African children saw their new schoolhouse, built by Rotary volunteers some 15,000 miles away in California. My wife and I have sloshed through the mud streets in India, Ethiopia, Turkey and Philippines giving polio vaccines to the children of the world. We have passed out food to starving people; given shoes to children who never owned a pair of shoes; and distributed worm medicine to children in remote orphanages. I had the opportunity to go to Bosnia and Croatia to deliver food, blankets, clothes and medicines for refugees fleeing from war torn areas. And no matter how hard we worked on humanitarian relief, we were ready for more.

You see, the message of our Christian faith is universal – happiness is enjoyed by both the *giver* and the *receiver*. There truly are blessings in giving as well as in receiving.

The story is told of a member of the English Parliament, who went to Scotland to make a speech late in the 19th Century. When his carriage became mired on a muddy stretch of road, a local farm boy brought his team of horses to the rescue. When the carriage was freed, the young boy would accept no reward because of his respect for the great Statesman. But the thankful official persisted, "Tell me, son, is there nothing you want to be when you grow up?"

"Oh, yes sir," said the boy, looking at the ground, "I want very much to become a doctor." "Then let me help you," said the Statesman, and that is what he did. True to his word, he made it possible for that young Scottish lad to attend a major university and eventually become a physician.

Now turn the clock ahead more than a half-century, when on another continent, another world Statesman lay gravely ill with pneumonia. The celebrated Sir Winston Churchill had been stricken while attending a wartime conference in the United States. The doctors recommended that they use a new "wonder drug" – called penicillin, which had been developed by a young doctor named Alexander Fleming. And soon Sir Winston Churchill regained his health. You see, Dr. Alexander Fleming was that young Scottish lad on the muddy road that day so many years ago; and the Statesman who had helped sponsor his medical education was none other than Randolph Churchill, the father of Sir Winston Churchill.

Oh, how many times do we discover that what we put into the lives of others comes back into your own?

I am sure that many of you could tell of your own experiences in discovering the fundamental truth of this message – your greatest moments of happiness are helping others.

But how can each of us live our faith – from Monday to Saturday?

Let me offer this simple and practicable suggestion. Give at least one hour of volunteer service each week and see if you don't find some new meaning in your life. Perform an act if kindness – just do something for someone which was never expected. Do something for someone – with no expectation of a return. I guarantee that you will find a kind of happiness you have never known. And if not, you will at least have surprised someone out of their wits.

I suspect you might be thinking, "Sure I would like to do that – but I'm too busy to volunteer an hour a week." But I am not suggesting that this be an addition to your busy schedule – it can become a part of your life. You see, we find time to eat, to watch television, to work, to sleep, to shop, to clean the house, to do the laundry or maybe play a ground of golf. What I am suggesting is if you want to put a new and real source of happiness in your life – take time to serve others. Just one hour a week – or just 10 minutes a day!

Look about you. There are tasks to be done. They are not all monumental tasks. Just do some random act of kindness.

Visit a lonely or shut-in person. Assist a library or museum. Give some canned foods to a food bank. Plant a tree or some flowers. Offer assistance to a school. Find a shelter for a homeless person. Collect used clothing for the needy. Clean up a public park. Deliver a meal to a forgotten friend. Phone some friends you knew 20 years ago and have been meaning to call them. Take some flowers to a neighbor. Give a contribution to a worthy cause. Help a youth group. Volunteer to do a job at the Church. Help a child learn a simple task. Teach someone to read. Offer to serve in a community dining room.

See, the list is practically endless – because the needs of the world are immense. But the rewards of joy and satisfaction for a more meaningful life are even greater – when you discover that Real Happiness Is Helping Others. That is putting our religious faiths into daily practice. It is so easy to do something unexpected for someone. Try it a week or a month – 10 minutes a day, one hour a week. I'll guarantee you'll have so much fun and your life will be enhanced more than you could ever imagine.

Let me close by asking:
- Do you hear the calls for help right here in this community?

- Do you hear children crying for food in our Bay Area?

- Do you hear the wailing of those who are suffering pain?

- Do you hear the muted voices of those who cannot read or write?

- Do you feel the anticipation of those who would be thrilled by a simple phone call?

- Do you hear the whispers of those who yearn for live or a caring word?

- Do you hear the hollow murmuring of those who are homeless or live in poverty?

- Do you hear the expression of anguish of those caught in the hopeless web of drug or alcohol abuse?

- Do you hear the muffled sound of those who dream of peace – but find there is no peace in the world or in their hearts?

Those are real calls for help. They are calls from children and adults – we may not know. They are the calls from the children of the world. They are calling all of us who care and have a faith based on love and the brotherhood of all peoples. They are calling us who wish to put real happiness into our lives – the kind of happiness, which merely comes from helping others.

Remember the words, which Jesus spoke: "What you do for the least of those – you do for me."

And we can do it – just one day at a time; one act of kindness; one act of love; one act of caring. Each night, pause for one moment and ask: "Did I put my Christian faith into action today?"

You will surely know if you did. I believe we can all put our Christian faith to work every day. If we make the effort, those good intentions of our faith, which we make on Sunday – can actually last from Monday till Saturday. Then, on Sunday, I'll see you in Church.

HELPING FRIENDS AROUND THE WORLD

(This speech was first presented in 2006 and 2007 to both The Rotary Clubs of San Francisco and Los Angeles for the annual meetings to which they invite the Consuls of other countries as guests. The presentation was subsequently modified and delivered to other clubs.)

It is a pleasure to speak on this very special day to honor the distinguished consulate representatives in our community.

Some of you may be very familiar with Rotary International, since clubs are found in nearly 200 nations and geographic territories of the world. You may have seen Rotarians conducting projects of humanitarian service or providing polio immunization in your country. Or, you may personally have assisted some of the 1200 Rotary University Ambassadorial Scholars or some of the 7000 Youth Exchange Students which Rotary clubs sponsor each year throughout the world. Rotary International is perhaps the most international organizations in the world. The very Object of Rotary encourages Rotary clubs to build better communities and help build a better world.

Rotary International just reached its 100th birthday – and this is a time when most people have retired or expired. But, I assure you that Rotary is alive and active around the world. During the time I served as the worldwide President of Rotary International, I had the opportunity to see thousands of Rotarians reaching out to help others in need. I have reached the conclusion that where the needs of the world are greatest – there you find Rotary service at its finest.

Shortly after I was selected President of Rotary International, a newspaper reporter from New York called me. He said, "I understand the Rotary International is an organization which works for peace, goodwill and international understanding." I said, "Yes, peace and understanding is one of our missions." Then he said, "Well, then, what do you intend to do about the situation in the Middle East?"

I replied that Rotary does not have the *weapons of war* – tanks, rockets, planes and battleships. Rotary uses the *instruments of peace* – food, water, medicines, education, shelters and those basic things which improve the quality of life. You see, there is more to seeking peace than the mere secession of hostilities – that is seeking a peace, which is measured by the quality of life in which people live.

As I have traveled in virtually every corner of the world, I have watched Rotarians engage in simple activities to enrich the lives of other people. Many years ago, I heard a story of a man walking along a mountain path. In the far distance, he saw *something* in the path. As he walked further, it appeared to be a *person* walking on the path. As he continued, he was sure that it was a *man* coming in his direction. As they came even closer, he discovered that the man was *his brother.* How often we observe people at a distance to be strangers, or persons of no consequence – but as we become nearer, we realize they are our friends or even our brothers.

That's the message of Rotary service. When we reach out to help others – new friendships are built, and simple mountain trails become paths to goodwill, understanding, and peace.

Rotarians provide "hands-on assistance" around the world

In Sweden, I met with the Rotary Doctor's Bank, a group of 60 physicians who voluntarily go each year for a month or two, to give their professional services to people in African nations, Pakistan, the Philippines and other regions – with no expectation of personal return, except the satisfaction of helping others.

In the South America nation of Colombia, I visited a very modern eye clinic, built by Rotarians, but serving hundreds of poor and indigent persons of Bogotá. Volunteer Rotary physicians perform surgery and ophthalmic services to children and adults – day after day.

In Johannesburg, South Africa, I visited a tuberculosis hospital overlooking the community of Soweto. The hospital had been in total disrepair before Rotarians led the task of rehabilitation. Now, daily care was being given to those with tuberculosis – from babies in cribs to adults learning trades, to assist them when their disease was arrested.

In Kuala Lumpur, Malaysia, we put on surgical masks and gowns to enter the Rotary Eye hospital. The patients, who would have to live in a world of blindness, were now seeing because of the work of volunteer Rotarian doctors who were providing cataract surgery.

In the Philippines, I was shown a building, located in a pocket of poverty, in which Rotarians provided about 150 small children a bowl of rice and a cup of soup day after day. And for many of these youngsters, this was the only meal they were assured.

In Rio de Janeiro, Brazil, I visited with young adults in a Rotary operated vocational school. For years this school has provided training in electrical repairs, auto mechanics, woodworking, dressmaking, food preparation, and electronic repairs. Not only do Rotarians support the skills training, they take the responsibility for finding jobs for the graduates who complete their training.

In Malta, I inspected a respite house for mentally and physically disabled persons – totally operated by Rotary volunteers and a small professional staff employed by the Rotarians. Each day, disabled persons are brought to this center in a beautifully restored mansion, to enable family members to have a few hours or a few days relief and rest from the arduous task of caring for their disabled family members. It was an amazing demonstration of caring and service.

I recall a hot summer day in Lagos, Nigeria when the Rotarians took me to a school for blind children. There were about 125 blind youngsters awaiting our arrival. We walked down the rows of children, perhaps 6 to 12 years of age. Then a young lad stepped forward and ran his fingers across a page of stiff paper, imprinted with the raised Braille writing. His little speech thanked Rotarians and The Rotary Foundation for a 3-H grant of $200,000 to purchase the first Braille printing press for the nation of Nigeria.

But, service to others does not always have to be huge monumental projects. In many instances, Rotary service is a rather simple act of kindness or meeting humble needs.

I have marveled at the Rotary sponsored reading program for children in Bangkok, Thailand. I have passed out bags of food for families in Mexico. I have delivered shoes and worm medicine to children in an orphanage in the Philippines. I have joined Rotary teams as they distribute hundreds of wheelchairs in China, Mexico and a hundred other nations to give mobility to the disabled who crawl on the ground or are unable to walk unassisted.

I have seen Rotarians drill water wells in villages around the world to give fresh water to a whole community.

These are not world-class events for the evening news-casters, but they are building friends and serving human needs wherever they happen.

When earthquakes strike, hurricanes hit, tsunamis destroy, and floods and fires consume the daily lives of people, Rotarians are frequently some of the first to offer aid and assistance.

The list of humanitarian projects being conducted every day in nearly every country of the world is almost endless – because the needs of the world are almost unlimited.

Without a doubt, Rotary's finest achievement has been our program called Polio Plus – a twenty-five year endeavor to eradicate polio in the world. The leaders of the World Health Organization, UNICEF and U.S. Centers for Disease Control have frequently stated that without Rotary International the achievements of polio eradication would have never occurred. When Rotarians launched the assault against polio in 1985, there were estimated 350,000 cases of polio in the world every year in about 125 nations. But, Rotarians have contributed nearly a billion dollars to secure polio vaccine, and donated millions of man-hours in conducting National Immunization Days. Today, polio exists in only 4 countries, and there are less than 1000 cases of polio each year. We are on the brink of eradicating this dreaded and life-destroying disease – and Rotary leads the way.

Now, I can't be absolutely sure that helping others around the world will build better friendship and form paths for peace. But in my opinion, *"trying is better than not trying."*

A few years ago, as President of Rotary International, I was in charge of the International Convention in Melbourne, Australia. At the opening session I designed a visual presentation, which told of the programs of Rotary service around the world. On the stage we immunized the 500 millionth child for polio. We had a woman from Uganda tell of how Rotary provided over 20 surgical operations after she had been mauled by a hyena when she was a child. We had a Rotarian who led in the care for a hundred thousand refugees fleeing from the war-torn areas of Bosnia. We told and illustrated the stories of Rotarians helping new friends around the world.

The next morning, under the door of my hotel room, I found this note, which had been written by an 18 year old Youth Exchange Student:

"Dear President Dochterman,
It is now 11:30 p.m. and I have just returned from the opening ceremony of the Rotary International convention. The performance at Rotary I saw to night was beyond measure. It was not only the actual work of Rotary International, but where the work comes from. It comes from the heart. It is given without hope for any personal reward, other than the satisfaction of knowing that real happiness is helping others. This amazes me.

I am 18 years old and have been an exchange student in Australia for 6 months. I do not know what vocation I will follow, but the program tonight made me sure of one thing – I must, at all costs, do my utmost to help my fellow humans.

I grew up in South Africa, and for the past 18 years I think the prejudices I have and seen are the basis for my humanitarian beliefs. Tonight, you put into words and picture everything I have always strived to express – but never quite managed. It was like my dreams coming true.

I have in the past believed that most things which man does on earth are rather futile, because evil always seems to triumph. This thought was proven completely incorrect tonight. I saw goodness, kindness and something so beautiful in action; my entire philosophy has been changed.

All I can say is "thank you" for giving me a glimpse of the other side – where sunshine is. I know I wish to follow the path, which leads to real happiness by helping others.

Yours in Rotary Youth Exchange, Gavin Russell"

Perhaps this young man said it best – Rotary works on the other side – bringing the sunshine where there is darkness.

So, when someone mentions Rotary International, just think – every hour of every day, Rotarians are bringing sunshine into the lives of new friends, most of whom we will never see or ever meet. But we know that some one's life may be just a little better because we are Rotarians.

In closing, let me tell one last little story, which possibly passed around the internet a couple years ago. A mouse looked through a crack in the wall to see the farmer and his wife open a package. The mouse wondered if this could be more food. But to his amazement and devastation, it was a mousetrap.

The mouse ran to the farmyard, proclaiming, "There is a mousetrap in the house! There is a mousetrap in the house!" The chicken clucked and scratched and said, "Mr. Mouse, I can tell this is a grave concern to you, but it is of no consequence to me. I just can't be bothered." The mouse turned to the pig and said, "There's a mousetrap in the house." The pig replied, "I'm sorry about that my friend, but I just can't do anything about it. But I'll put you in my prayers."

The mouse turned to his friend the cow and said, "There's a mousetrap in the house." The cow replied, "Wow, I'm really sorry for you, but it is not really my problem."

So, the mouse returned to his nest in the house to face the mousetrap alone. That very night a sound was heard throughout the house like the sound of the mousetrap catching its prey. The farmer's wife rushed to see what was caught. But in the darkness, she did not see that it was a venomous snake whose tail was caught in the trap.

The snake bit the farmer's wife, and he rushed her to the hospital. She returned home with a high fever. And anyone knows that you treat a fever with chicken soup. So, the farmer took his hatchet to the farmyard to get the chicken to put in the soup.

The sickness continued and tragically the farmer's wife died, so neighbors came to the funeral. So, the farmer had to go to the farmyard to butcher the pig and slaughter the cow to feed the guests.

The mouse peeked through the crack in the wall and was so sad to see what had happened to his friends.

So, the next time that you hear of the problems and concerns of people you haven't met, – and you think that they don't concern you, – just remember, when anyone is threatened by poverty, sickness, illiteracy, homelessness or despair, – we may all be at risk.

In this world we all call home, our lives are woven together in an amazing fashion – so, let's remember that the concerns of people anywhere, should be a concerns for all of us.

That's the mission of Rotarians – doing what we can to build better communities and reaching around the world to build goodwill and understanding through friendship and service.

That is why Rotarians reach out to friends around the world and why we value so highly the friendship of the diplomatic leadership of the world.

WHEN DID YOU BECOME A ROTARIAN?

[This has been one of my favorite speeches for Rotary club meetings. It has been given to dozens of Rotary clubs and district conferences throughout North America for over 20 years.]

On occasions such as this, I frequently ask, "When did you become a Rotarian?" And they will say, "Oh, I joined Rotary in 1985 or I joined five years ago." Then I have to say, "No, that wasn't my question. I didn't ask when you joined a Rotary club, I asked – when did you become a Rotarian?" You see, there is a huge difference.

I've known members who belonged to a Rotary club for years, and they never became Rotarians. And there are some people who were Rotarians long before they joined a Rotary club.

A real Rotarian is a person who takes special pride in his or her business or profession. You can count on them to be fair and honest. Their word can always be depended upon. They are always willing to step forward when help is needed. They will always show up at the club functions. They give support to The Rotary Foundation every year. They give encouragement to the club president and the committee leaders who are doing their best to make the club interesting, alive and relevant. That is a *real* Rotarian.

Service Above Self is not just a Rotary motto to hang on the wall – it is actually a way of life.

My friend, the late Skip Kreidler from Tulsa, Oklahoma, used to tell a story which he said happened in the Houston Rotary Club some years ago. Houston used to be the largest Rotary club in the world and they had some of the most prominent executives in the city as members. The Houston Club had a community service committee, which helped people in need throughout the city. One member had frequently been asked to assist with some of the community service tasks, but he was always too busy.

On this particular day the club president called Tom and said, "We have an urgent need to help a single mother down in the Spanish speaking section of our city. She has a seriously ill son who has to go to the county hospital. We would appreciate it if you would take on this task." Tom said, "Hey, don't you know I'm a busy person. I've got a large company to run – and all these people depend upon me. I don't have time to take some kid to the hospital." The president replied, "Tom, we have asked you time and time again to do a job for Rotary, but you are always too busy. If you don't start doing your part, I think I better spend the rest of the year drumming you out of this club." Tom relented and grudgingly said, "Okay, nobody ever quite explained it that way before. What's the job?"

An hour later, Tom found himself in a part of town he had never seen. He went down dirty streets among old buildings and finally found an old tenement house. He parked his car and trudged up two flights of stairs. In the dingy hallway light he found the room number and knocked on the door. A small Mexican woman answered. She was carrying an infant in her arms. Through the open door he could see a small boy lying on the well-worn sofa. He explained that he was sent to take the boy to the county hospital, and went in and rather gingerly guided the sticky fingered youngster down the stairs to his car.

He put the child about as far as he could over by the door in the front seat, and started for the county hospital. They had driven only about a block or two when the small brown-eyed youngster looked up and said, "Mister, are you God?" Tom was startled and answered, "No, boy, why do you ask that?" "Well, Mister, my momma was on her knees praying for God to help us, when you knocked on our door."

Tom could think of nothing else as he drove on to the hospital. He checked the boy into a four-bed ward, and glanced around the room at the sad faces and tears of the three youngsters in the other beds. He left the hospital and went to his car.

But Tom didn't go back to that busy office where everyone was depending on him. He drove down the street to a toy store and picked out some fluffy teddy bears and stuffed animals. Then he drove back to the county hospital and gave each of the four youngsters a new stuffed animal and teddy bear. He stood a moment and watched the tears on the youngsters faces turn into smiles and laughter.

Then he still didn't go back to that office. Tom drove to a grocery store and filled two large sacks with bread, milk and other food and went back to that old tenement house. He walked up the two flights of stairs, knocked on the door and gave that lonely mother, caring for two other children, the sacks of groceries.

Finally, Tom went back to his office. He picked up the phone and called the Rotary club president. He said, "Mr. President, do you know how bad the poverty is in some parts of our city? There are people who are hungry and sick and nobody cares! It's about time our Rotary club gets involved. Mr. President, you appoint a committee – but make me the chairman!"

When did you become a Rotary club *member* – and when did you become a *real Rotarian*? Did you ever call your Rotary club president and say, "There is a job to do in our town – and I'm ready to do it!"

Many members become Rotarians the day they discover that Rotary adds something special to their lives. Some people become Rotarians the day they volunteer to rebuild a community playground. Others became Rotarians when they took disabled youngsters to a day at the zoo or taught them how to catch a fish. Some became Rotarians when they lifted a person who had been paralyzed by polio, stroke or birth defect and placed them into a Rotary donated wheelchair. Has anything ever happened to you that caused you to say, "I think today I became a Rotarian."

I can tell you it is a rare experience to pass out food to a person who is starving. It is something special to see a child receive a pair of shoes – who had never owned a pair of shoes before. It is an amazing sight to see a blind person receive the gift of sight because a Rotarian provided for cataract surgery.

Perhaps one of the most touching experiences a Rotarian might have is to give the two drops of polio vaccine to a child, held by his or her trusting mother – and you know that child will never have the prospect of being paralyzed or even death from polio. And this has been done for over two billion children of the world as a result of our Polio Plus program. That is over 99 percent of all the children in the world – touched by Rotary's commitment to eradicate that horrible disease.

Mary Elena and I have participated in National Immunization Days in many parts of the world – in India, Turkey, Philippines, and Ethiopia. Perhaps one of the traumatic events occurred in Addis Abba Ethiopia during the opening ceremony before we sloshed through the mud roads in the poverty-stricken villages.

A ceremony was held to start the Day of Immunization. The President of Ethiopia was present to give the drops of polio vaccine to about one hundred little youngsters as they walked down the aisle toward the head of their nation. Just at that time on the other side of the room were about 35 little youngsters in wheelchairs, leg braces and crutches – all tragic victims of polio. These children, with their bent backs, twisted legs and withered arms sang a song to the President of their country. It went something like this, "It's too late for us, but don't let other children get polio. It is too late for us. Do what you can to kick polio out of Africa." Yes, it was too late for those youngsters – but it was not too late for other children who received the two drops of polio vaccine that day. That has been the magic of Rotary's Polio Plus program.

I recall a day when I was in a Nigerian village in Africa and watched fresh water being pumped out of the ground – for the first time. For generations the women had carried water in buckets for over a mile from a polluted stream. Now, Rotarians had placed a water pump right in the middle of their little village of grass huts. The pump had become the center of the entire village. The women gathered around the pump, washed clothes and sang songs as children ran around, as kids like to do. A woman was saying something as we had a little dedication ceremony for the pump. I asked my translator what she was telling me. He said, "She wants you to know that when Rotary built the well, their children stopped dying." The Rotary Foundation contributions made it possible to sink the pump – but more importantly – to save their children.

The dollars you gave to The Rotary Foundation provided grants to enable blind persons to see. You provided shelters for the homeless, cleft palate surgery, wheelchairs for those with no mobility, medicine and malaria nets and school equipment where education is so limited. As I traveled the world, I've seen these celebrations, which come from Rotarians meeting human needs. Watching the tears of joy are occasions you never forget. When Rotarians work to meet the basic needs of mankind – food, health care, clean water, sanitation, education, and relief from poverty – you realize these are the instruments to bring peace into the world. Rotary works for peace through our Rotary Foundation and through our many acts of World Community Service.

On the other side of our Rotary Foundation are the many kinds of educational programs. About twenty years ago, a young lady from India came as an

Ambassador Scholar to the University of the Pacific, where I was the Executive Vice President. She was studying to help young people who had speaking and hearing disabilities. Lalitha Prathap was a charming person who enjoyed the friendship of all of the Rotary Clubs in the area. On the campus she was well known, as she wore attractive saris and always had a cheerful smile. When the year ended, I learned that she was asking several Rotarians if they could help her find a sponsor in order for her to stay in the United States. I suggested that I would visit with her and discuss her plans.

So, Lalitha came to my office. I said, "Lilitha, I am pleased that you had a wonderful experience here at the University and found your studies valuable in the United States. But, Rotarians in India sent you here to study and return to your country. You have an obligation to the people of India." Lilitha had tears in her eyes and replied, "Oh, I thought you would help me." "No," I said, "You go home and help the people of India. You have been given a great educational opportunity – now you must use the Ambassadorial Scholarship in the way it was intended." So, Lalitha returned to India.

Although I kept in touch with Lalitha, and her husband and children, for a year or two, but I eventually lost touch. So, that could be the end of the story.

However, a few years ago, I was in Bangalore, India for a Rotary assignment. As part of that trip, the Rotarians had scheduled me to attend a dedication of a Rotary sponsored 3-H grant which provided a pacemaker bank at a hospital for very poor and indigent patients. The cardiac hospital served both adults and children. It was a grant, which I had approved as chairman of The Rotary Foundation trustees. There were two or three hundred people gathered for the dedication ceremony at the hospital. There were lots of flowers and banners and a plaque was to be unveiled to indicate Rotary's involvement.

Just before the ceremony began, the District Governor said I want you to meet the chief administrator of the hospital. And to my surprise, it was that former Rotary Ambassadorial Scholar, Lalitha Prathap. We sat together and visited a bit. With tears in her eyes she recalled that day nearly 25 years before, when I had advised her to 'go home and help the people of India.' She slipped a small gift into my hand and said, "Thank you for what you did for me that day, and thank you for the work of The Rotary Foundation and for all it has done for me and the people of India. You have given me so much." You see, Latitha had become one of the outstanding leaders in all of India caring for children with disabilities. To this day, she continues to give her talents to help the people of India.

The activities of The Rotary Foundation are like a pebble dropped into a lake or stream and the ripples go on and on. You never know where the ripples of your Rotary dollars will go and who they will touch.

That is why it is such a proud moment when you can say, "I think today I became a Rotarian – not just a member of a Rotary club."

Well, I think I have talked about as long as it seems.

So, I will close on a personal note. As the worldwide President of Rotary International, the theme I selected was "Real Happiness Is Helping Others." I truly believe that when you help others something very important comes back into your own life. There are people, right in this community, who need your Rotary club. They may be hungry; they may be hurting; they may be cold; they may be friendless or live without hope of a better life. But, when Rotarians reach out and touch their lives, our lives will be so much better.

In my message, as I traveled the world, I frequently quoted an old Chinese proverb:

If you want happiness for an hour – take a nap.
If you want happiness for a day – go fishing.
If you want happiness for a week – take a vacation.
If you want happiness for a month – get married.
But, if you want happiness all your life – it will come only by helping others.

So, my message to every Rotary member, if you want to be a real Rotarian, do some good things right here in your own community, or even reach to someplace around the world. There are people who need you. You can bring happiness and you can improve the lives of people you may never know or ever meet. But you can be sure that you can enable someone, somewhere to have a little better life. Helping others, in my opinion, is the real meaning of Service Above Self.

I assure you, the day you reach out and do some random acts of kindness, or work with fellow Rotarians on a worthwhile community project, will be a special day in your life. And that will be the day you can say, "Today, I think I became a *real Rotarian*."

COTTON CANDY ROTARIANS

[This speech was first written in 1984 when I was Vice President of Rotary International and President Carlos Canseco selected as the theme "Discover a New World of Service". The speech has been revised numerous times to emphasize that there is so much more to Rotary than going to meetings, enjoying lunch and listening to a speaker.]

Ever since I was a child, I have had a fascination with the circus. I love a circus, with its parade, big tent, the animals, clowns and sideshow entertainers. I remember that fantastic day when I attended my first circus. We followed the parade and milled with the crowd. I'm sure I had never seen anything quite so exciting. What a thrill it was for a six-year-old youngster to see the Greatest Show on Earth.

As I recall, we stopped at every sideshow. I couldn't imagine a man swallowing flaming torches; death defying motorcycle riders; a man in a cage of deadly snakes; and seeing a man lying on a bed of spikes. Maybe we even saw the world's tallest midget. Oh, there were peanuts by the bag, and most of all, huge cones of pink cotton candy! I could have watched the sideshows for hours with absolute fascination.

But, then we pushed past the midway of these spectacular wonders, and to my amazement, we entered the big tent. Wow! I discovered a whole new world of entertainment!

There were dozens of clowns and flying trapeze performers. I saw elephants and wild tigers, acrobats, prancing horses and dancing bears. The ringmaster announced one extravaganza after another. There were tight ropewalkers and a man shot from a cannon. For a six-year-old boy, there was nothing like discovering the circus big top. To this day, there is an excitement in the music of the calliope and the rolling drums announcing that the big show is about to begin!

With this personal reference to my secret love of the circus, you might wonder how this relates to Rotary International.

First, you can have a lot of fun at your weekly Rotary meeting – just seeing friends and listening to an interesting program. But there is so much more to Rotary when you discover that the main events are actually going on inside the big top. So many members never know that these are happening.

Just as my first experience at the circus, it is possible to enjoy the sideshows so much that you don't even realize that there is a much bigger show going on inside the big tent! I see so many Rotary friends enjoying the cotton candy and the peanuts they find before they ever get inside the main tent that they never discover there is a whole new world of Rotary going on – and they are missing it all.

Some Rotarians are proud of their long history of 100% attendance; they enjoy the weekly lunch with some friends; have a laugh or two – but never discover how much of the world of Rotary they have never seen. Oh, there is nothing wrong with being a cotton candy Rotarian and enjoying the side shows of our weekly meetings – but, somehow they have missed the really big show. Rotary can be the Greatest Show On Earth!

Rotary is an amazing worldwide organization. We have immunized over two billion children of the world against the dreaded disease of polio. But, have you ever thought about participating in a National Day of Immunization in the heart of Africa? Some Rotarians are doing that and discover a new world of service. Some Rotarians may volunteer to spend a weekend rebuilding a school for impoverished children, or rebuilding a community playground in Mexico or Central America. They see a new dimension of Rotary service.

Rotary sponsors about 8000 Rotary Youth Exchange students to live in another country for a year. Have you ever volunteered to spend a day with a Youth Exchange student in your club? Have you thought about getting involved in the high school Interact Club or spend a day at a RYLA camp? Some Rotarians work with local schools; help with a drug abuse prevention program; or take part in a club's outing for children with physical disabilities.

Some Rotarians become involved in literacy programs to help people learn to read – and there are many such people here in our community. Medical and food supplies are collected for food banks and health clinics, or are being shipped to remote areas in the world.

There are Rotarians experiencing the emotions of delivering a wheelchair to a person who crawls on the ground or has no means of mobility. Others provide prosthetic limbs or hands to those who have little hope of ever receiving such devices. There is a whole big world of Rotary out there – which most Rotarians never discover.

If a person is to be a Rotarian, there is no reason that they should not know what their organization is doing. There is a job for every Rotarian. It doesn't have to be on the other side of the world. It doesn't have to be a monumental one. There are opportunities for service right in our community.

There are schools, which need volunteers. There are youth groups and teams, which need leaders and coaches. There are shut-ins who need visitors. There are community facilities, which need repair. There are streams, which need to be cleaned. There are clinics, which need assistance. There are food banks, which need food. The list is practically endless. These are the services which Rotarians can provide as they talk about *Service Above Self.* These are the activities you find in the main tent of Rotary.

There is a whole new world of Rotary to be discovered by most Rotarians. If you really want to get more out of your Rotary membership, let me make one suggestion. Start today and give at least one hour of volunteer service each week just because you are a Rotarian. At your club meetings give a report on your volunteer service. I guarantee that in no time at all your Rotary membership will have an entirely new meaning.

Or, maybe you will just perform one act of kindness each day – something that was never expected. Just do something for someone with no expectation of any return. If you do one unexpected act of kindness for another person each day, you will find a kind of happiness and satisfaction you have never known before. And, if you don't, you will at least have surprised someone out of their wits.

The point of this message is simply this. To be a Rotarian is to have fun and enjoy the weekly meetings with your friends in Rotary. That's the cotton candy of Rotary – so enjoy it!

But, don't stop there. Come on into the big tent of the Rotary world and discover the Greatest Show on Earth. The drums are rolling. The calliope is playing. The Ringmaster is ready. The Rotary show is going on – so don't miss it!

It's time to discover a whole new world of service, and you will find it inside the big Rotary tent!

OPPORTUNITIES, CHALLENGES AND RESPONSIBILITIES OF AN INTERNATIONAL ORGANIZATION

[This speech was prepared for the 50th anniversary of the signing of the United Nations Treaty and delivered at a conference sponsored by Rotary International in San Francisco in June, 1995.]

This is an intriguing topic assigned to me by the conference committee. As I approached the theme, I felt it was important to separate the terms, *opportunities and challenges*, from the word, *responsibilities* of an International organization. The opportunities of, and challenges to, an international organization largely relate to the hopes and dreams of the organization to build a world of peace, goodwill, harmony, tolerance and understanding. These are the common hopes of virtually every international organization.

On the other hand, the *responsibilities* of an international organization depend largely upon the nature or characteristics of the organization itself. The responsibilities of a governmental international organization may be quite different from the responsibilities of a volunteer international service organization. Let's explore these challenges, opportunities and responsibilities.

If our goal is peace and goodwill among peoples of the world, how can it be achieved? Obviously, peace may mean to some, merely the secession of warfare or the absence of military conflict. This type of peace is almost entirely in the hands of governments and governmental organizations. The peace which comes from the elimination of military conflict is the challenge to the peacemakers and peacekeepers of national and multinational military forces.

However, there is another kind of peace, which is more than the sheer secession of hostilities. This kind of peace is the *quality of life* in which humans live. If our challenge is peace, goodwill and world understanding then our efforts must be directed to enhancing the quality of life in every corner of the globe. What is the challenge for this type of peace in the world?

In my opinion:

A world half starving and half over fed will never be a world at peace.

A world half sick and half healthy will never be a world at peace.

A world half illiterate and half educated will never be a world at peace.

A world half enslaved and half free will never be a world at peace.

A world which condones drug abuse, senseless violence and unpunished crime will never be a world at peace.

A world of prejudice, intolerance and distrust will never be a world at peace.

At the recent Rotary International Convention in France, I asked a Nigerian Rotarian, "Why is there so much civil war and conflict throughout Africa?" He commented, "When people are hungry, sick, and have no hope, there is a tendency for them to fight just to get a better life – and war becomes inevitable." At the same time a Rotarian from Tanzania stated that in his opinion, "The three B's are really the agents of peace – bread, bedding and basic education."

If these statements are true, it means that the international organization which is seeking peace and goodwill among people will depend upon finding:

Food and water for the hungry and thirsty;
Medicine, vaccines and medical care for the sick;
Education and learning for the illiterate and uneducated;
Human freedoms for those who live in bondage;
Tolerance for all to worship; and
Respect for all races and cultures.

If this is the challenge and opportunity, whose responsibility is it to try to fulfill these needs throughout the world?

The immediate answer might be – the governments of the world are the ones who have the resources and strength. But, we know that is not always the case. We are all aware of the tremendous differences between the capabilities of the highly industrialized nations and the slowly developing nations of the world.

National governments may try – but national governments alone will not achieve the human peace the world seeks by using their military forces.

To a large extent we must look to the combined governments – as represented in the various units of the United Nations.

If we take this analysis one step further, we may see that there is still a very significant role and responsibility for non-governmental international organizations. The search for peace is a historic goal and dream of Rotary International.

Governments approach to conflicts frequently resort to the *weapons of war* – tanks, battleships, rockets and planes, as well as economic sanctions and international blockades.

Rotary International works with the *instruments of peace* – food, clean water, education, medical care, friendship, and all of the resources which improve the human condition of those who live in poverty, hunger, ignorance and fear. Realistically, we must recognize that where conflict and strife is rooted in economic, military, political, and historic ethnic confrontation, the task of bringing a lasting peace may seem overwhelming. On the other hand, the peace which comes from world understanding and goodwill is the process of Rotary and many other non-governmental organizations. I truly believe that these tools of peace are, and will always be, the only means to find a just and lasting peace in the world. History clearly shows that after the military truce is reached, the first and major task is to rebuild the nations by meeting the human needs of the people.

I am convinced that Rotary's instruments of peace – tolerance, education, food, clean water and sanitation, basic medical care, aid to children and the disabled – these are powerful tools which can and will bring ultimate peace in the world.

For centuries, the great philosophers, theologians and statesmen of the world have dreamed of a world at peace. The great thinkers and leaders of all time have talked about a world in which people could live together in tolerance and harmony. Such a society would respect all religious beliefs and not be disrupted by frictions based on color, races, cultures or ethnic backgrounds. Such a society would actually care about other people – those who are sick, homeless, hungry, illiterate, disabled, helpless and poverty stricken.

The amazing thing is that such an international organization has been created – we call it Rotary International. The members of this worldwide organization come in all sizes, shapes, races, creeds, colors, religions and lifestyles. They have been molded into one organization to serve others. That is the noble idea of Rotary. Is it possible that Rotary International is really a microcosm of that society of concern and caring which mankind has sought for generations?

For ninety years, Rotary has demonstrated that people can live, work, share and serve together. This is true even with all the differences of philosophy, religion, language, customs, skin color, and political orientation. Even with all of these differences, it is possible to have a one-world organization committed to the friendship, cooperation and volunteer service, which leads to peace.

I must admit that on occasion, even this highly ethical and idealistic organization may occasionally fall short of its full potential. Not withstanding those shortfalls, certainly the world needs what Rotary *says it is* – an international organization, which reaches out into the world with a program of peace, goodwill and hope.

Clearly, the greatest responsibility of an international volunteer organization is to be what it *says it is* – and then strive to achieve all of it great potential. A true international service organization has the responsibility to help those who are unable to help themselves.

As I dream of the great opportunities for and challenges to Rotary, I suspect that our greatest shortcoming is that we think too small. Our dreams and goals may not be great enough. Our vision may not be broad enough. If we fear the risks of failure – we will never embark on the tortuous road to world peace.

When Rotary International leaders first adopted a suggestion, thirteen years ago, to eradicate polio in the world, we were amazingly naïve in understanding the magnitude of the task. But, even though our Polio Plus program became much larger than anyone ever visualized, Rotarians have not retreated from the goal. For our future, we must see new visions, which will stir the energy and enthusiasm of every Rotarian. A world organization today must dream big dreams. Then, we must never lose sight of our goals.

Can you dream of building a two or three billion-dollar Rotary Foundation Permanent Endowment fund to underwrite and expand the educational and humanitarian activities of our Foundation? Can you imagine a project to sink a hundred thousand water wells, and sanitation facilities, and water collection basins – all for the purpose of bringing fresh water to the parched areas of the world? Can we create a distribution system for the huge surpluses of food in the world to be shared with those who live in hunger – perhaps using the military planes of the world? Could you dream of Rotary offering a fifty million dollar prize for the discoverer of an AIDS or cancer vaccine?

Could our dream include a plan to supply vaccines and medicines to control all the preventable diseases, which wrack the minds and bodies of children who live in pain and misery? Can you dream of a project to expand educational opportunities to every village and nation in the world? Would Rotary accept a challenge to plant a billion trees to enhance the quality of our air and environmental atmosphere? Are we capable of creating an effective plan to eliminate drug abuse, crime and terrorism, wherever it exists? In your wildest imagination, can you see Rotarians leading a program to seek religious and political tolerance throughout the world?

Such an idea may be immediately dismissed as impractical and absurd. However, if non-governmental organizations are to be major instruments for peace in the world, we must have dreams of great magnitude – dreams which stir the sole of all mankind.

A dream must be more than a wishful thought. We must work to transfer dreams into actions. Over fifty years ago, Rotary's founder, Paul Harris, commented, "I have no hesitance about dreaming about the future of Rotary as long as we dream good dreams and then work to make them come true." This is just as true today as it was fifty years ago. We must dream good dreams, great dreams, far-reaching dreams – then work to make them come true.

I would be remiss on this occasion of recognition of the United Nations, not to make one more comment about our efforts to seek peace in the world. We must not be afraid of risk. We must be willing to raise our voices with courage.

Clearly, Rotary and other organizations may not be political in nature. However, we must never hesitate to speak out to world leaders in the cause of peace. The leadership of non-governmental organizations must never hide our outrage when we observe senseless killing of the youth of our nations, as well as defenseless children and civilians. Let us use every ounce of our influence and persuasion to seek the end of terrorism and violence. Let us speak out in every language and to every world authority – that all mankind needs and yearns for peace.

Let me conclude by saying that the greatest opportunity, the most significant challenge and most taxing responsibility of an international organization is to *be what it says it is* and *to do* what it has the capacity of doing. If our dream is of a world at peace, we must work to make it happen. That is the *challenge* to Rotary International. That is the *opportunity* for every international organization. And more importantly, it is a *responsibility* from which we must not retreat.

ROTARY'S TRANSITION INTO WORLDWIDE SERVICE

[In 2008 I was invited to give a speech at the Rotary International Convention in Los Angeles to review some of the history of Rotary's transition from local club activities into worldwide humanitarian service. This is the speech I prepared for that occasion.]

I suspect that the only reason I was asked to speak this morning is the fact that our founder, Paul Harris, died in 1947, and they wanted someone who has been around about as long. Yesterday I saw someone in the hallway who said, "I heard your last speech." I said, "I'm not so sure that it was my *last* one." And he said, "Well it should have been." Obviously, it is a great pleasure to be here, since Paul isn't around.

Today we are exploring some of the history which shows how many of Rotary's programs and activities have evolved into the fabric of this great organization. Throughout our history, most of the great programs of Rotary grew out of a simple idea created by the activity of a single club or in the mind of a creative Rotarian. Simple ideas can be a powerful thing.

In the early decades of Rotary, a Rotary Club in Elyria, Ohio created a "crippled children's committee" which eventually led to the National Easter Seal Society to help children with injuries, birth defects or crippling diseases. In the 1920's virtually every club had a "boy's work committee" which enabled Rotarians to become one of the largest sponsors of Boy Scout troops. Rotary's Youth Exchange program grew out of the activities of French and German Rotary clubs wishing to build new friendships following World War I. Upon the death of Paul Harris, a series of scholarship awards were created to honor his memory. Those first 18 scholarships established a pattern for the nearly 50,000 Ambassadorial Scholarships, which have been awarded since 1947.

During our first fifty years, Rotary service activities were largely done by individual Rotary Clubs selecting projects in their own communities. However, a major change took place during the 1960's as clubs began to look at the whole world as their community – and international service activities began. In 1963, Rotary President Carl Miller introduced the Matched District and Club program. Shortly after, in 1965, The Rotary Foundation launched the very first Matching Grants for humanitarian service. The following year, in 1966, the concept of World Community Service was officially launched. Rotary service gradually became *international* in scope. In 1967, Rotary expanded its international activities with the Rotary Volunteers Abroad by offering technical and professional assistance to communities in developing nations.

Refugee aid given to Bangladesh in 1971 and earthquake relief to Nicaragua in 1973 were other additions to Rotary's growing extension throughout the world.

But Rotary leaders dreamed of doing even more. In 1978, the Health, Hunger and Humanity program was initiated by RI President Clem Renouf, which enabled Rotary to complete international projects much larger than any club or district could ever attempt. For the first time Rotary International began to support large scale projects which could really make a difference in the world.

As Rotary celebrated and collected funds for its 75th anniversary, the 3-H program was launched, and the very first project was to provide polio immunization to six million children in the Philippines. This effort, and other successful immunization projects, led to the Polio Plus campaign to eradicate polio throughout the world. And that story, alone, identifies Rotary with one of the world's greatest humanitarian achievements. Other 3-H projects provided community sanitation in Colombia; national literacy programs in Thailand; health care and food production projects in several nations. Rotary was funding higher levels of international service.

At about the same period, Rotarian Tony Zino, in the Manhasset Rotary Club on Long Island, New York, read of a child badly mauled by a hyena in Uganda. He was so touched by the tragic plight of Margaret-Rose Illukol, that he initiated an effort to help her secure the plastic surgery she needed. That volunteer surgery was ultimately found in Australia. But, this simple act of kindness set the stage for a Rotary initiated program called Gift of Life. In 1974, a second child, five year old Grace Agwaru traveled from Uganda to New York to undergo a four hour open heart surgical procedure to close a small hole in her heart chambers. These simple responses by Rotarians developed into a dynamic worldwide program, which has provided the Gift of Life to over 10,000 children, involving more than 60 worldwide Rotary districts. This Rotary initiated crusade to help children with life threatening heart defects and other medical conditions has opened many other doors of Rotary sponsored steps towards international goodwill and peace.

In a remote community of Jaipur, India, in 1968, Dr. Pramod Karan Sethi, and a local sculptor, had an idea that many amputees and persons with birth defects could be given a chance to walk if an inexpensive prosthetic device could be designed. With plastic pipe and scrap rubber the amazing lightweight Jaipur Foot was created. Today Rotarians have provided a Jaipur foot to over 100,000 men, women and children to whom new mobility, independence and dignity have been given.

There are so many other Rotary initiated programs, which started when a few Rotarians saw a need and reached out to meet it.

When a group of Texas Rotarians, led by Rotarian J.B. Roberts, learned of the desperate famine among the Tarahumara Indians in Central Mexico, they turned to another sponsored Rotary project, the Breedlove Dehydrated foods in Lubbock, Texas and shipped thousands of pounds of dehydrated food to Mexico. This humanitarian response led Rotarians to create Hunger Plus, a new Rotary sponsored relief agency to reduce hunger and develop new food supplies. Since 1998, this program has provided Rotary club sponsored shipments of millions of meals of dehydrated fruits and vegetables to nearly every continent in the world to relieve hunger, malnutrition and offer disaster relief.

In England, Rotarian Tom Henderson had an idea that one box, filled with lifesaving materials and equipment could be prepared and instantly ready to be sent to areas facing disastrous floods, earthquakes, tornados, tsunamis, and other disasters. Thus, the Shelterbox program began. Each Shelterbox provides a tent and supplies for 10 persons with cooking equipment, sleeping bags, basic tools, a water container and other essential items. This program, started by one Rotarian as a club millennium project has been continued by Rotarians, and has spread around the world to enable Rotary clubs to provide immediate disaster relief to over half a million people in more than 30 nations, because Rotarians care.

As the years passed, and with the experience gained in our Polio Plus program, many Rotary clubs and districts found that their efforts could be greatly expanded by working with other humanitarian agencies and Non-Governmental Organizations. A major leap was achieved in 2000 when RI President Frank Devlyn established Task Forces to create working partnerships with organizations, which offered unusual opportunities for Rotarians. We have seen hundreds of Rotary clubs developing relationships with other humanitarian agencies.

For example, it is estimated that 50 million people live in blindness or limited vision for lack of cataract surgery or care for basic eye diseases. By cooperating with several of the leading world agencies, such as the World Health Organization, Global Vision, International Trachoma Initiative, and other agencies, plus support from several world-wide pharmaceutical companies, Rotarians have created an active program, aptly named

Avoidable Blindness. With 3-H grants and matching grants, Rotary clubs and districts are caring for millions of people afflicted with river blindness, cataracts, trachoma, lack of corrective lens, and other forms of vision problems. Rotarians alone have sponsored over a half million-cataract surgeries throughout the world. What a tremendous demonstration of the new directions in Rotary's world community service.

In another outreach of Rotary service, over 2000 Rotary clubs and districts have donated over 200,000 wheelchairs in 100 countries of the world in cooperation with the Wheelchair Foundation, established by Rotarian Ken Behring in California in 200l. These Rotary clubs have given mobility to children and adults who were victims of polio, birth defects, disabling accidents and disease. Many of these Rotarian sponsored distributions have been enhanced by Rotary Foundation Matching Grants in cooperation with the Wheelchair Foundation, operating in Canada, England, Australia, Florida and California. Through these cooperative efforts, over 200,000 people are living a better life because Rotarians saw a need and filled it.

In more recent years, we have seen the creation of a new area of international service – the Rotarian Action Groups. This activity grew out of the long established Rotary Fellowships of Sports and Recreation. The new Rotarian Action Groups are initiating worldwide activities and awareness in such areas as Population & Development, Elimination of Malaria, Blood Donations, Multiple Sclerosis, Polio Survivors and several other humanitarian activities.

One such activity is the Water and Sanitation Action Group, which is seeking and supporting long-term water initiatives for the 1.2 billion people who do not have safe water and the 2.4 billion who do not have proper sanitation. It is estimated that over 7000 Rotary clubs are already engaged in water projects. This Action Group, working with WaterAid, Water for People, Global Water Challenge, Living Waters of the World, Engineers Without Borders, Canadian International Development Agency and many Churches, Foundations and agencies, is promoting clean water and sanitation for millions of people in 40 countries in Africa, 25 nations in Asia and 17 countries in South America.

Another Rotarian Action Group is facing the worldwide devastation caused by AIDS. Rotarians have reacted to the plague of this deadly disease with a variety of educational, medical and care giving activities. In one single project, the AIDS Action Group is providing care and support for 46,000 orphans and vulnerable children in Africa. Working with USAID, and in partnership with several corporate foundations, the Rotarians of the AIDS Action Group are extending their work in a pilot project in Kenya and other nations throughout the African continent. Clearly, Rotarians are giving education, medical care and hope to the children and youth of Africa.

Oh, there are so many more fantastic projects which Rotarians are supporting to distribute medical equipment, establish blood banks, build schools, construct shelters, improve sanitation, control disease, provide micro-credit, remove land mines, enhance literacy, plant seeds for food, restore dignity, assist refugees, and simply bring hope to the world. The list of Rotary projects in the past 50 years is almost endless – because the needs of the world are almost unlimited.

We have shown the world – and we have proved to ourselves – that Rotarians can meet even greater challenges by multiplying our resources and working with other organizations and foundations, which share common humanitarian goals. Rotary can *share* with other organizations; Rotary can *share* with other volunteers, and Rotary can *share* with the world.

The real message I have this morning is that there is so much more to Rotary than meeting and eating. The world needs Rotary. Sadly, there are many Rotarians and Rotary clubs who have not yet discovered the real joy and satisfaction, which comes when we share our time, energy, and resources with the people of the world. Don't just let your Rotary club stand on the sidewalk and watch the parade go by. If you are going to be a real Rotarian, get on the bandwagon and be part of the parade yourself!

Rotary's greatest days are still to come! Our greatest ideas may be in the minds of Rotarians in this room today. Our most exciting achievements may come when you and your club get involved.

Rotary's achievements of the past are merely the prelude to the Rotary of the future. Rotary has the potential to build better communities and build a better world. And would you believe it – it is all up to you, because you are some of the most fortunate people in the whole world – you are Rotarians.

REFLECTIONS ON THE ROTARY INTERNATIONAL PRESIDENCY

[At the end of my year as worldwide President of Rotary International, I was asked by many Rotary clubs and District Conferences to tell about the experiences of the presidency. This speech was prepared in 1993 and revised on several occasions. Obviously, the membership figures and other numbers were from the original address.]

So many of you have inquired what I am doing since I have ended the amazing year as President of Rotary International. Frankly, I have been faced with some unusual withdrawal symptoms.

As some of you know, during the year as RI President, I only spent five nights in my own bed – four nights for the Christmas Holidays and one night to see my tax consultant.

The first thing which happened – the mail stopped. There was so little mail our postman thought that I had moved. The only mail I have to read are K-Mart ads and offers for time-shares in Salina, Kansas.

Some days I go over to the airport – just to stand in line. Last week I went to a Rotary Zone Institute, and it was the first time in a year that I had to ride the back of the plane – and they even ran out of peanuts before they got to my seat.

Next, the phone calls stopped. Nobody wanted an official Rotary appointment. Yesterday I talked ten minutes to a wrong number. I subscribed to a 900-phone number, called "Dial A Crank." Each morning you just call the number and someone will yell at you for something.

I joined an adult quilting class – just to find something to do with all those little club banners I collected around the world.

And I have so many souvenirs from my travels – my house looks like an "up-scale flea market."

I have received some wonderful gifts from generous Rotarians. There is nothing like a beautiful Waterford crystal serving bowl – with a Rotary wheel and the District Governor's name engraved on the side!

I'm still introduced at my own club as a *Visitor*. Last week I had to pay for lunch for the first time in a year. Even one member of my club asked me, "Have you been away?"

You really know that your year as President is over when you go to a Rotary Convention and see your theme pins were being sold at half price. And even more, your theme banners were being used as packing materials. By then, you know you really are a *Past* R.I. President.

Well, I had better say something – since I ate the lunch.

During the year as President of Rotary International, I met dozens of Rotarians who said, "You are the first real live Rotary President I have ever met, so I just wanted to shake your hand."

I realize that the worldwide President of Rotary is usually just a picture on the cover of the July issue of <u>The Rotarian</u> magazine. To most Rotarians, the presidency is a very remote position. There is little reason to know much about the R.I. President, and even less chance of hearing about it.

Since I really am a live person and have just completed the very unusual experience as the world president of our organization, I'll tell you a few things, which may be of interest. Perhaps this will give you a better understanding of Rotary itself.

First, let me tell you how a Rotarian actually becomes the world president of Rotary International. Rotary actually exists in 187 different countries and geographical territories. We have over 26,000 clubs and over one million, one hundred and fifty thousand members. Everything we do must be put into an international perspective. Every decision, every action takes into account various languages, different cultures, different economic consequences, different traditions and different perspectives. Rotary is not a United States organization – with members in other countries. Rotary is a world organization – with over two-thirds of our membership outside the United States.

As we talk about the presidency, we must realize that only once in every three years is the R.I. President selected from the United States. Looking over a five-year period, we had presidents from Brazil, India, USA, and next the president is from Switzerland and then England.

The selection process for the president begins with a Nominating Committee of 17 members selected from all areas of the world. They all have been past directors of Rotary International and are free to pick any person in the world who has served as a District Governor and a R.I. Director. So, they have about 150 potential candidates.

The Nominating Committee meets and selects the nominee, after at least 10 members agree. Then the tradition is to call the person who has been selected and each person on the Committee asks if he will accept the presidency. It is similar to lighting striking, and you are standing under the tree! There is a waiting period for other candidates to "challenge the selection" which is a complicated process I am not going to try to explain. Eventually the nominee is presented to the next Rotary International Convention and it is ratified by voice vote.

I was selected as the 82nd president of Rotary International. The selection took place in September, 1990 and I was not to take office until July 1, 1992. So, it gives you about a year and a half for preparation. The work started almost immediately. Planning becomes an all-consuming task.

First you think about the areas of emphasis you want to put on the programs for the year. Then you begin to think of a theme for the year. Ever since 1950, the R.I. President has created a theme around which the program was built. I thought of many ideas which were fairly short, and hopefully somewhat motivational and helpful to club and district leaders.

In one early speech, I kiddingly told Rotarians that I was considering the theme, "Honk If You Love Paul Harris." In no time at all, I began receiving bumper strips, T-shirts, ball caps, and other items from Rotarians around the country – printed with that theme!

In selecting the theme, one must consider how it can be translated and understood in various languages. Some visuals must be designed and symbols must be checked to assure that in some cultures the designs are not offensive. However, I finally selected "Real Happiness Is Helping Others," and gave an idea for a design to the graphics team of Rotary.

Then I selected a jacket color. Since 1984, the District Governors and senior leaders of Rotary have worn a special sport coat which identifies the group. I selected a red jacket for two reasons. It is very distinctive and had not been used in previous years. And because red is considered a very happy, lucky and successful color in many cultures. It just seemed to fit in with the theme of real happiness.

Then I started thinking of special events for the year. I thought that three Presidential Conferences of Goodwill and Development would be appropriate in Barcelona, Spain, Johannesburg, South Africa and at the United Nations in New York. Then I planned sixteen "salutes" to the programs of Rotary to give opportunities for Rotarians in sixteen major cities to meet and talk about the work they are doing in such areas as drug abuse prevention, hunger programs, Rotary Village Corps, literacy, youth exchange, vocational service, inter-country committees, Ambassadorial Scholars and so forth. This concept was to enable Rotarians of the world to talk directly to the R.I. President and demonstrate the success of our many activities.

Then there were travel schedules to arrange. Nearly all of the 365 days on the calendar were fully committed before the year began. Planning began for the training of the 501 District Governors at the International Assembly for their tasks of leadership. This week-long training is the "quality control" for Rotary International around the world.

At the same time, the President-elect attends many committee meetings, as well as meetings of the R.I. Board of Directors and the Trustees of the Rotary Foundation, in order to be brought up to full speed in the matters of consequence to Rotary.

Finally, July 1st arrives, and you are the world President of Rotary. It is an awesome responsibility to be the head of a world organization. You take residence in Evanston, Illinois and move into the big office on the eighteenth floor of the Rotary world headquarters. There is a lot of symbolism at the headquarters on July 1st. The photograph of the new president is posted in the building. The national flag of the president's native country is raised in front of the building. The executive staff formally meets and greets the president. A picture of the new Rotary Board of Directors is quickly placed on the wall. There is no question – a new president is aboard and a new year is underway.

The new Rotary President becomes Chief Executive Officer of a $55 million dollar operation. There is a staff of 500 persons and 9 branch offices in various parts of the world.

Almost immediately you begin a travel schedule, which never stops. Even though you are on the other side of the world, you are still in full charge of this world organization. You expect to receive you daily supply of FAX – maybe 15 or 20 pages of items which only the president is expected to consider and decide.

Quickly, you are in the process of planning the International Convention, the site of which has been decided about six years earlier. The Convention is fully the responsibility of the president, and no major decision is made without his concurrence.

You have responsibility for four meetings of the R.I. Board of Directors – the eighteen member governing body of Rotary. These meetings usually last one week and the agenda may include 150 to 200 items, covering every conceivable topic about Rotary you can imagine.

At the same time, the president is selecting the 501 personal representatives to attend each of the Rotary District Conferences to be held around the world. Amid all of this activity, is the constant travel of the president – who has already received invitations from perhaps 700 or 800 Rotary clubs to attend club, district, zone and regional meetings. For example, there were 175 clubs celebrating 75th anniversaries during the year – so I decided I would attend only one – the first club which invited me – York, Nebraska.

In planning your travel schedule, you try to go to certain countries which the previous presidents have not recently attended. It is expected that the president will go to many of the major cities of the world. But, you also pick some areas where the R.I. President might be helpful in giving encouragement to the Rotary movement. I went to such places as Poland, Malta, Nigeria, South Africa, Turkey, Estonia, Russia, Croatia, Malaysia and Spain; as well as fifty other nations.

The travel is exhausting. Meeting new people every day – and these people have been sleeping in their own beds. You haven't been in your own bed for months. The president must be friendly, smiling, interested, and alert on every occasion. You are not supposed to get tired seeing Rotary projects, never get sick, and never have a cold. You are their president, and this is the only time many of the Rotarians will ever see a real president.

Generally, Rotarians take very good care of the president. No one wants anything to happen while the president is in their country. Usually some special arrangements are made to travel through airports, immigration and customs with no hassle. Often there will be police escorts through traffic. Armed security is occasionally visible if it seems appropriate to the local situation.

It is customary for the R.I. president to meet, if at all possible, with heads of state and national media in every nation he visits. This takes time and there is usually lots of protocol and briefings. I occasionally concluded that this is mainly of benefit to the local Rotarians who love to have their pictures taken in the presence of their king, prime minister, national president, lord mayor or some other high ranking official. But, it also demonstrates the very high regard that heads of state hold for the world organization of Rotary.

During the year, I visited such officials as the Prime Minister of Japan, King of Thailand, King of Sweden, Presidents of Greece, Argentina, Guatemala, Honduras, Estonia, Philippines, South Africa and a dozen other countries. In addition, there were many mayors and high officials in the major cities I visited. Most of these events required a presentation of a Rotary gift – all of which I had to carry in my luggage.

Finally, you arrive at those final months of the year, and it is almost time for the Rotary International Convention, which was held in Melbourne, Australia. It fulfilled all of my greatest dreams. The Convention Committee planned for attendance of 18,000 persons, and the final registration exceeded 23,000. I believe all of these attendees left the Convention very proud to be Rotarians.

As I look back over the year, I would make two or three final observations:

First, Rotarians come in all sizes, shapes, colors, with various cultures, religions, languages, and life styles. But with all these differences, they are brought together by the simple desire to help other people and to build friendship and goodwill around the world.

My second observation is that the work of Rotary is done by an amazing small percent of the Rotarians in the world. This doesn't mean that the majority is not comprised of good and wonderful people – it is just a realistic conclusion that a huge proportion of the Rotarians in the world don't have the slightest clue what Rotary International is all about or what it is doing. For a majority of our members the meaning, value and programs of Rotary seem to be a total mystery.

They really only know what goes on at their own club meetings.

I have met Rotarians who couldn't tell a Group Study Exchange Team from a Rotaract Club. I am astounded that there are so many Rotarians content to have their membership measured merely by attending meetings, eating lunch and enjoying the friendship and weekly programs. Certainly, I am not critical of these members. They are some of the finest people on earth, and I respect them as fellow Rotarians. But somehow, they have not experienced or captured the real thrill of Rotary in action.

It remains a challenge for Rotary leaders to motivate and encourage all members to realize that there are millions of men, women and children in every part of the world who live a life of poverty, sickness, hunger, illiteracy, homelessness and indeed hopelessness – and they need Rotary.

A third observation is that our greatest challenge is to remain a totally *international organization*. This may seem naïve, or even contradictory, when we consider that Rotary is perhaps the most international organization in the world today. Internationality is perhaps our greatest strength. However, I see many subtle and unintentional influences challenging our worldwide unity. With regional trade agreements, nationalization, common markets, currency collaborations, the evolution of new regionalization and other developing spheres of influence, it would be easy for a world organization to become fractured, split and dispersed in its mission. I also see so many Rotary clubs totally consumed in their local community concerns, that they close their eyes and minds to the internationality and world perspective of Rotary. They seem to be missing so much.

Rotary's destiny depends upon maintaining our international unity as a single organization united in local and worldwide humanitarian service and committed to a world of friendship, goodwill, tolerance, respect and concern for all peoples. So, my plea is that as Rotary looks to its future, we must continue to *think* internationally, to *act* internationally and *be* truly inter-national.

So, those are some of my reflections of the past year. It is an incomparable experience. I have frequently thought that I have received so much from the experience that my only hope has been that I have been able, at the same time, to contribute some things of lasting value to Rotary International.

With this amazing year of unusual experiences behind me, I now return to my own Rotary club, where they will be entrusting me with the job of Assistant Bulletin Editor. Thanks to the Rotarians of the world for giving me these great months to remember.

THE STORY OF ROTARY RIBBONS

[It is traditional that ribbons indicating the offices held or formerly held by Rotary leaders are attached to their name badges at Rotary International Conventions, International Institutes and other major international meetings. This short speech was a little routine, which I first presented at an International Institute and on a few other occasions where the audience is familiar with Rotary ribbons.].

Some of you may be attending a Rotary Institute or Convention for the very first time, and consequently are extremely impressed by the blaze of Rotary Ribbons.

Perhaps you have even been mystified by the meaning and significance of ribbons. Frankly, I have been appalled at how little attention the subject of Rotary ribbons has been given in the curriculum of our recent leadership training at Presidents Elect Training Seminars and International Assemblies. For generations, ribbons have been a significant element in the culture of Rotary International.

Rotarians enjoy ribbons. In fact, Rotarians have a passion for ribbons. In some instances, that is the only passion they have.

You will certainly amaze your fellow Rotarians – as well as non- Rotarians wandering through the hotel lobbies – if you can demonstrate your knowledge of ribbon significance.

First, let me say how important it is just to wear a ribbon. If you have no ribbon at all, people will assume that you are really nobody. Convention attendees will wonder why you are here and totally ignore you. If you are wearing no ribbon, people will walk on the other side of the street just to avoid you. Occasionally – dogs will bark. I've seen Rotarians kick sand in the face of a person with no ribbon.

In some instances, I have watched Rotarians pin their name badge at the top of their necktie – just to make people think that they are actually wearing a long and multi-colored ribbon.

So, as part of the educational program of this Institute, let me review some of the exciting history and tradition of Rotary ribbons. Actually, Rotarians are judged by the color, number and length of the ribbons they wear.

Generally speaking, incoming Rotary officers wear a white ribbon – such as incoming club presidents and district governor nominees. White signifies virginity and purity. These individuals are totally unencumbered with any worthwhile factual information. Don't ever expect to receive correct information from a person wearing a white ribbon.

Next are the blue ribbon persons. A blue ribbon is a symbol of being in 'first place.' It is similar to the blue ribbon given to the head hog at the county fair or the top dog at the kennel show. A blue ribbon person would never think of wearing brown shoes with a dark blue jacket. A blue ribbon is the sign of a person holding a very important position or one who has been appointed to serve on a vital committee. Never mess with a blue ribbon wearer.

Occasionally you will see a purple ribbon. This is a strain of royalty which only befits an international president or past president. Some Rotarians assume that a purple ribbon is the same as a blue ribbon – which has faded by too many years in the sun. A purple ribbon is a true sign of someone who has been to the top. Usually you will find a purple ribbon person sitting at the side of the room in a wheelchair – just mumbling about how things used to be, and of course, drooling a lot. An aide frequently walks by and wipes their chin.

A gold ribbon is truly the sign of aging. It means that you once had an important job – but it's all over. Gold ribbons – please don't call them yellow ribbons – are for past District Governors, and former R.I. Directors and Trustees. A gold ribbon person is considered a – RIPE – Rotary International Past Executive. When you have a gold ribbon you are certainly listed in Rotary's giant book, Who Was Who.

A red ribbon is a symbol of urgency. You are on the Rotary staff, or a Sergeant-at-Arms, an Aide or performing some very vital assignment. A red ribbon is Rotary's equivalent to a phone call to 911. If something goes wrong, they want you to find them quickly. Hence, the red ribbon actually symbolizes a tongue hanging out – a mark of total exhaustion. Red ribbon people have all the correct answers – but seldom slow down long enough to hear the questions.

Green ribbons are for those who seem to know a little about everything – they are environmentally sound and politically correct. They are generally reserved for Rotary International Assembly instructors who seem to know more and more about less and less.

Once in a while you will see a rather ominous black ribbon. It is a sign of mourning. A black ribbon usually means that you are a task force member – and nobody has asked you a question or called upon your obvious expertise. If you see someone with a black ribbon, do me a favor – ask them a question on just about anything.

A pink ribbon is a mark of a real 'nobody.' The pink ribbon means that you have never been given a job – but you just like to wear ribbons.

Ribbon identification is a Rotary tradition

The second part of the Ribbon system of hierarchy is the *number* of ribbons you wear.

If you have no ribbon at all – all Rotarians will simply avoid you. That is why it is good to have some kind of ribbon – even if you have to make one from some old Christmas wrapping.

When you wear one ribbon – everyone recognizes that you are on your way up in Rotary. One ribbon demonstrates that you have been a club officer, or became a Paul Harris Fellow – or somehow got elected to an important job. Some Rotarians will do strange things just to get one ribbon.

With two ribbons, the person at the registration desk might recognize you. Not your name, of course, but they may have seen you at a previous meeting. A two-ribbon person can readily talk with a one-ribbon person. Two ribbon people usually sit in the first row of the meeting room, hoping to be seen – even if not identified.

If you have three ribbons, people will assume that you can recite the 4-Way Test and probably have at least been a sergeant-at-arms or an aide to an important Rotary officer. A three-ribbon person may soon become an RI Director – or perhaps even have been one. With three ribbons a few people will recall your name – without looking at your name badge first. Three ribbon persons usually sit near the air conditioning system – so that the breeze will flap their ribbons.

The four-ribbon person is either bringing ribbons from previous conventions, or is really moving up in the Rotary world. This is the person who knows the actual boundaries of your district and has spoken personally to the RI President more than 30 seconds outside of an elevator. The four ribbon person talks freely to a three-ribbon person – if there is no one else in the room.

When you get five ribbons, you can probably name at least three current RI Directors. With five ribbons, you are frequently mentioned in the Governor's monthly newsletter. People walk across the room just to shake your hand. Your mother-in-law complains that you are putting far too much time into Rotary.

The five-ribbon person occasionally receives an internet copy of letters to an RI Director and easily carries on conversations with three and four ribbon persons. These persons frequently take old issues of *The Rotarian Magazine* to leave in doctor's offices and barber shops.

A six-ribbon person becomes very special. Without question he or she will own a personal copy of the *Rotary Official Directory* and a *Manual of Procedure*. This person is on a first name basis with the RI President and is occasionally asked to appear on panels at Zone Institutes. By this time it is no longer necessary to speak to persons who have less than three ribbons. You now have so many ribbons that only the top one can be read. It is quite possible that all the other ones may be blank.

When so many ribbons are piled high on a name badge, it is surprising what the unseen ribbons may actually say. I remember one year seeing Past President Chuck Keller wearing a ribbon he had won in a fifth grade kite-flying contest. A six-ribbon person usually is talking with another six ribboner – and occasionally a five-ribbon wearer.

Now, a seven-ribbon person is almost unheard of. You can see people, from a distance, asking who they are. The seven-ribbon person is often a President's Representative to a District Conference and most of their clothes have been purchased from Russell-Hampton. Clearly, the seven-ribbon man can talk with God. And if you have eight ribbons – God talks back!

And with additional ribbons, the only person who talks with you is Frank Devlyn. Frank talks with everyone!

In some cultures the length of the ribbon has significance and historic meaning. Some Rotarians place great importance in the order in which the ribbons are hung from the name badge. However, because of time, I will refrain from that detailed explanation.

Many Rotarian leaders wear jackets, which are color compatible with their ribbon collections. Some Rotarians frame their ribbons after a convention. Others collect them and place their trophies in safe deposit boxes. Some have been know to sell them at Rotary fundraising auctions, or even offer them for sale on E-Bay.

So, that is about all you really need to know about the theory and historic meaning of Rotary ribbons to be socially acceptable at a Rotary International Convention.

Just remember, if Paul Harris had not created Rotary International a hundred years ago – at least someone would have invented Rotary ribbons. Any questions?

ROTARY CHRISTMAS COMMENTS

[On many occasions, I have been asked to speak at Rotary luncheons or dinners during the Holiday Season. These are the comments I made in 1998 at a Rotary Christmas party.]

Before I make a comment about the season, I want to share an important, although rather sad, note I received by E-mail today from Santa Claus, North Pole dot com:

> I'm writing this letter to tell you
> That taxes have taken away
> All the things that I've needed,
> My reindeer, my workshop, my sleigh.
>
> So, I'm making my rounds on a donkey,
> Old, and tattered, and slow.
> So, if you don't see me this Christmas,
> You'll know, I'm out on my ass in the snow!

Now, with this bit of Holiday sentiment behind us, let me make just a few comments about Rotary and the spirit of this wonderful season of the year.

The annual Holiday Season is a time for sharing. We share and exchange gifts; we enjoy gathering with family and friends; we offer greetings and good wishes to all. We hang colored lights in our homes and on the streets – and their glow radiates out to friends and strangers alike. It is a season when we talk of peace and goodwill. We reach out to those less fortunate and share our gifts and blessings.

To a large extent this is the same message and mission of Rotary. Just as we cannot be in Rotary without friends around us – it is difficult to enter this season alone. We want to share the Holidays with others. Rotarians want to share experiences with our friends – those we know and enjoy each week – as well as with those we may have never met.

It is too bad that the spirit of Christmas goes by so rapidly. We often spend weeks preparing for the Holidays. There are stacks of greeting cards, we send and receive. The Christmas tree goes up and all of the brightly colored lights and balls are hung with so much care. The stores are filled with the music of Christmas carols, colorful decorations, and frantic shopping. Kids line up to visit the department store Santa Claus. The Salvation Army bells tinkle on the streets. Holiday parties are planned. Stockings are hung by the fireplace. Homes are filled with combinations of Holiday aromas – pine needles, fruitcake, gingerbread, homemade fudge and a roasting turkey. Families gather to open presents and go to church services.

And the amazing thing is – it will all be gone in a few days. And you know it is over because we are immediately flooded with year end sales and the endless string of football bowl games!

Fortunately, Christmas and this Holiday spirit can be a part of our life as Rotarians every day, if we really try. There is no limit on helping others. We can feed hungry people every day. We can provide clothes, health care and education for someone every day. We can extend our circle of friends and build goodwill every day. Around the world, some Rotarians are maintaining this Holiday spirit every day.

It was the author, Henry Van Dyke, who was asked if it were possible to keep the Christmas spirit all year long? He put the whole message in these words:

"Are you willing to forget what you have done for other people, and to remember what other people have done for you? Can you ignore what the world owes you, and to think what you owe the world? To see that our fellow-men are just as real as you are, and to try to look behind their faces to their hearts, hungry for joy...to close your book of complaints against the management of the universe, and look around for a place where you can sow a few seeds of happiness...Are you willing to do these things, even for a day? Then you can keep Christmas.

Are you willing to stoop down and consider the needs of little children; to remember the weakness and loneliness of people who are growing old; to stop asking how much your friends love you, and ask yourself whether you love them enough; to trim your lamp so that it will give more light and less smoke; and to carry it in front so that your shadow will fall behind you...Are you willing to believe that love is the strongest thing in the world...stronger than hate, stronger than death...and the blessed life which began in Bethlehem nineteen hundred years ago is the image and brightness of the Eternal Love? Then you can keep Christmas. And if you keep it for a day, why not always?"

As we enjoy this Holiday Season, I hope all of us realize how fortunate we are to be a part of this wonderful world of Rotary. We have the opportunity to keep the Christmas spirit all year long through our many activities of giving and sharing.

May your Christmas and Holiday Season be a merry one. Enjoy these days with the same enthusiasm you did as a child, and I promise you that the spirit and happiness of this wonderful season will slip into your heart and stay forever.

That is my Christmas dream.

ROTARY MEANS OPPORTUNITIES

[Occasionally I have been asked to talk about the meaning of Rotary. This speech was originally delivered in 1990 at a conference of District 5220 in Sparks, Nevada and subsequently expanded and updated.]

Describing what Rotary means to me has been a real challenge. This is especially true when one realizes that Rotary has been an important part of my life, as well as my family's, for over 50 years. As a matter of fact, it is difficult to recall the days when Rotary was not a part of my daily routine

As I pondered this question, I thought of the hundreds of experiences we have had at club meetings, Rotary conferences, International Conventions and traveling to far places to see Rotary in action. I recall dozens of community projects, Youth Exchange students, drives home late at night, rushing to a speaking engagement, fund raising activities, international committee assign-ments and well over 2600 club lunches – every week for over 50 years. Rotary has almost become a regular habit.

When I tried to put the meaning of Rotary into a single word, I kept coming back again and again to one word – OPPORTUNITY. Rotary offers opportunities beyond your wildest imagination.

Joining a Rotary club guarantees you nothing. There is no assurance that you will enjoy Rotary or that your Rotary membership will benefit you in any way. Rotary doesn't give money-back guarantees. Rotary only offers opportunities – the rest is up to you. You can either take them – or you can pass them by. Opportunities only knock – they don't kick in the door.

So, what are some of these opportunities, which might enhance your life – if you heed the knock on your door?

The first opportunity of Rotary is to create some of the closest friendships in your life. Without Rotary, I would never have met Bill Ives, a member of the Detroit Rotary Club. We met in 1983 when we became members of the Rotary International Board of Directors. The friendship we and our wives developed has been one of the rare dividends of Rotary. Bill served as Aide to the President during the year I was given to serve as President. We have shared many travels, exhausting days, and endless laughs. Hardly a week goes by that we do not visit by phone and share a unique kind of respect and confidence built on Rotary friendship. Without Rotary, I would never have known some very personal friends, such as Carlo Cortopassi, Fred Joyce, Lou Piconi, Heywood Norton and other Rotarians who are as close as any family members could ever be. Through Rotary, our circle of close friends has extended to Japan, Australia, New Zealand, England, Brazil, France, South Africa, Switzerland, The Philippines, Mexico,

Argentina and dozens of other nations. My address file lists hundreds of friends who would otherwise be unknown – except for the magic of Rotary friendship.

Lasting friendship is one of the opportunities for Rotarians

Rotary friendship is a special kind of relationship. I will never forget the dark day when my wife, Dorothy, died. A Rotarian came to my home. He sat and talked for maybe two or three hours – the time did not seem to matter, even though he was an extremely busy person. I assure you that in life's darkest moments, the rare friendship of Rotary can mean more than any words can describe. I've often wondered if I ever adequately told Joe Serra what his Rotary friendship meant to me on that dark and dismal day in 1987.

A second opportunity which Rotary offers is to discover new experiences in community service. I happened to have been elected president of the Berkeley Rotary

Club as it was planning its 50th anniversary. That club was not only an old Rotary club of 225 members; some of the members themselves were getting pretty old. It was particularly challenging to me, since I was only the second president who had served while still in his thirties. We decided that we would place an art and garden center in one of the city parks. After many city council meetings, we were finally able to convince the city fathers that we had no ulterior motives and that our gift had no strings attached. A prominent Rotarian architect generously donated all of his professional services – my job was to raise $50,000 from the Rotary club members. In the early 60's, raising that kind of money from club members, who thought giving a five-dollar contribution was a big deal, was not an easy task. The old timers in the club thought I was out of my mind.

So, I decided to visit the senior member of our club, Les Hink, the third generation owner of Hinks Department store, and told him the story. For a young guy like me visiting Mr. Hink, was like an alter boy seeking an audience with the Pope. He listened, and finally this nearly fifty-year member of Berkeley Rotary Club looked straight at me and said, "Do you really think that you could get the members of Berkeley Rotary to support a project like that?" I gulped and answered, "Well, if I could get 100% participation, I think we can do it." Les Hink leaned forward across his big desk and said, "OK, son, if you THINK YOU CAN, you're half way there. Count on me for the first $500 bucks!"

So, it went, week to week – donations from one member at a time. I was concentrating on 100% participation and the goal of fifty thousand dollars. Finally, we were down to the last member – we had support from

224 of the 225 members. We had reached our dollar goal, but we were still short one member participating. This last member clearly could afford a contribution, but he just did not like the idea of making a gift to the city. Finally, two of us went to visit the reluctant member. We asked, "Won't you give us just one dollar so that we can say this is a project supported by 100% of the club?" He didn't budge. As we were about to leave, I commented, "I'm not sure if your fellow Rotarians will respond or not, but at next week's meeting I am going to ask that we take up a collection in your name for our anniversary project. It won't be easy to raise a dollar, but we will give it a try." He reached for his wallet, and we left with one dollar and had 100% participation.

But the important thing was, as we dedicated the new Berkeley Rotary Art and Garden Center on our 50th anniversary day – that member who so reluctantly gave a dollar, was standing in the front row enjoying the pride of seeing our Rotary club doing something important for the community.

I mention this story because it illustrates so many different kinds of projects which Rotary clubs can undertake to build better communities. There are dozens of needs throughout every community. A Rotary club can meet many of these needs, and all it takes is to seize the opportunity. I learned from that experience long ago, that *if you think you can do it, you are half way there.* I also learned that the whole club enjoys a successful project. That is the opportunity to serve your community.

A third opportunity which Rotary offers is the personal reward of touching lives of people you may never see and will never know.

It was a hot afternoon as several Rotarians crowded in a car as it bumped along a dusty road in Lesotho, South Africa. We were looking at schools being used in the backcountry for the children of the Zulu tribes. About every ten miles we would come to a clearing where there were several buildings serving as schools. Actually, they looked more like long chicken coops. After seeing a half dozen of these school shacks, we came upon a clearing with new concrete block buildings and corrugated steel roofs. This was a new school – clean, sturdy and very functional. But the impressive thing of all was the sign above the door – Built by Rotary Clubs of California; the Rotary Club of Livermore and Rotary Club of Stockton. And, of course, there was the Rotary wheel.

As we experienced the emotion of seeing the name of Rotary so far away from home, around the corner of the building came a chorus of about fifty little Zulu children – their black faces shining; their white teeth gleaming; their freshly laundered shirts spotless and their bare feet stomping in the dust. Many of these youngsters had walked three or four miles on dirt trails on a school holiday to say "thanks" to a couple strangers from the United States, some 15,000 miles away – just because they came from Rotary, the people who built their new school. Each of you would have felt the same pride we had that moment.

Without that opportunity of Rotary, how would we have ever heard those beautiful voices or learned how Zulu children express their sincere appreciation for a service project by people they would never see or ever know. This is the kind of Rotary opportunity, which comes when members get involved in a World Community Service project, matching grant, 3-H project or a Polio Plus immunization day. These projects stretch your club membership around the world.

A fourth Rotary opportunity is to learn and experience some of the cultures of the world.

Some years ago, I was representing the President of Rotary International at a District Conference in Kaohsiung, on the southern tip of Taiwan in the Republic of China. As our police escort delivered us to the entrance of the gigantic cultural center of the city, we could see the huge building about a quarter of a mile in the distance. As we looked up the long stone sidewalk and courtyard filled with fountains, there were four thousand Rotarians lining both sides of the walkway. A youth marching band led the way, as we headed a procession of local dignitaries. With a crowd of four thousand Chinese, two astonished Caucasians were being treated as if they came from royal blood – rather than two common folks from Stockton, California.

However, besides all of the fascinating experiences of that three-day submersion in this unusual foreign culture, there was another part to the story. After the conference ended, we flew to Hong Kong for a 12-hour layover, before connecting to a plane to New Zealand. Unfortunately, the people whom we had expected to meet us in Hong Kong had somehow failed to receive our travel schedule. So, we stood bewildered in the airport luggage area figuring how we would handle our 12 hour layover.

At that moment, two of the Hong Kong Rotarians, who had been at the Rotary conference in Kaohsiung came through the airport and stopped to speak to us. When I explained that we had somehow missed connections with our hosts who were to meet us, they quickly said, "You are now OUR guests for the day." From that moment, John Yuen and Peter Hall put aside all of their personal affairs and for the next twelve hours entertained us to every possible sight or private feature of Hong Kong one could imagine. Their *life* became *our* life – just because we were Rotarians.

International friendships, whether they come through Rotary Youth Exchange programs, Group Study Exchange Teams, Rotary Friendship Exchanges, volunteering for international projects, Twin Clubs, or International Conventions, can all open giant doors for new Rotary experiences. Truly, the world can shrink to very small dimensions when we take advantage of the wonderful friendships that result from worldwide Rotary opportunities.

Oh, how I wish we could slow down our daily pace and remember that our hours are going by so swiftly. We are passing one Rotary opportunity after another. How often we have said, "We should plan to get involved on one of those international activities. We ought to do something. We want to take advantage of the worldwide resources of Rotary." But next week comes along. Well, maybe next year we will have more time. And before we know, the Rotary opportunity has gone forever.

The final opportunity I'll mention is the chance to experience the real happiness which comes when you discover and accept the opportunities of cheerful service.

That great philosopher, physician and African missionary, Dr. Albert Schweitzer, who incidentally was a Rotarian, said it this way one day when he was talking to a group of people, "I do not know what your destiny will be; but this I do know; the only ones who will find true happiness in life, are those who have searched and found how to serve others."

The rain pounded on the windshield of the car as lightening flashes lit up the rows of sugar cane lining the mud-covered roadway in the heart of the Dominican Republic. I had arrived, hot, tired and exhausted at midnight and was being escorted on a two-hour drive to the tiny village of Azua. My volunteer task was to evaluate a proposed 3-H project to help Rotarians establish a vocational school in this remote area. My Rotary host, one of the few people who spoke English in Azua, tried to help me struggle with my modest Spanish language ability. I had taken those classes in my college days quite a few years before. I kept remembering those Spanish phrases, "is this the way to the bull ring; my pencil is yellow; I left my umbrella on the bus," but could never seem to work them into the conversation. Frequently, there were long pauses in our conversation as I tried to think of a word we would both understand. The temperature was around one hundred degrees, the humidity was stifling and sheer fatigue seemed overwhelming.

It was during one of these conversational lulls that a strange thing happened – perhaps you have had the experience when the same thought comes to two people. The thought in my mind was, "What in the world am I doing here in the middle of the night in this remote countryside of the Dominican Republic?" The thought expressed by my traveling host was, "What a strange occurrence that you are here. You have traveled all across your country on a Saturday night when families should be together; you came across the Caribbean

Sea to my little country. You are coming to my poor village because you care about the people of Azua. That is what Rotary service is all about." He reached over in the darkness and shook my hand and said, "Gracias, Cliff, gracias." And from that moment there was never a question in my mind why I was in the Dominican Republic. I was there because *Rotarians care*.

We reached the village about two o'clock and I was shown to the little room which was to be my quarters. I sat on the edge of the cot and soon an amazing thing happened – I no longer felt exhausted. I felt an excitement, exhilaration, and a strange feeling of satisfaction. In the dim light from the tiny bulb hanging from a cord, I could see little lizards scampering about, but somehow it really didn't matter. Those words kept ringing in my ears – "You came here because you care about the poor people of Azua. That's what Rotary service is all about." And I remembered again that message of Dr. Schweitzer – "The only ones who will be truly happy are those who have searched and found how to serve others."

My friends, if you want to put real happiness in your life, look for opportunities of Rotary service. Rotary is the mechanism to become a more vital, interested, active person. In Rotary we learn to accept strangers as new friends. In Rotary we learn to listen patiently to another person's point of view or hear about subjects we never thought would interest us. In Rotary we learn to be compassionate to and considerate of the needs of our community or in some poverty stricken part of the world. In Rotary we find the lasting satisfaction of serving others without the slightest expectation of personal return.

Those are some of the great privileges of Rotary. And they are your opportunities because you are a Rotarian.

I have one final story. I have been told that there was an old railroad in the deep South, called the Critchfield Railroad. One day the train was slowly rolling down the track. A crew of laborers was working on a siding. As the train slowly passed, a well-dressed businessman was standing on the platform of the train's caboose. The businessman recognized one of the workmen and called out, "Hi, Charlie, how's it going?" Charlie waved back and yelled, "Howdy, Joe, things are great. Thanks for asking." The fellow workman inquired who that important man was on the train platform. Charlie answered, "That's Joe, and he is the president of the railroad." "Well, how did you get to know the president of the company?" Charlie thought a moment, then said, "Joe and I came to work for the railroad on the same day over thirty years ago." "But why is he the president of the company, and you are still here working on the rail crew?" "Well, I'll tell you," said Charlie, "Thirty years ago I came to work for one dollar an hour – and Joe came to *work for the railroad.*"

How many people join Rotary just to be a member of a Rotary club? And how many join to take advantage of the wonderful opportunities to become a Rotarian?

Have you discovered the opportunities? Opportunities for life-long friendships. Opportunities for life changing service to others. Opportunities to get involved. Opportunities to enrich our very existence. Opportunities to find a kind of happiness we have never known.

These are the opportunities we can find in Rotary – and they are ours, just for the taking. So, what are we waiting for?

WINDOWS TO THE WORLD

(This is my favorite address about The Rotary Foundation. I prepared it when I was Chairman of the Trustees of The Rotary Foundation in 1997-98, and gave the speech at the Rotary International Assembly and the International Convention in 1998. A video which was made at the Convention has been used by many Districts and Clubs as a description and promotional piece for The Rotary Foundation.)

To most Rotarians, it is unnecessary to review the fascinating history of our Rotary Foundation. You know how one Rotarian, named Arch Klump, suggested back in 1917 that Rotary establish an endowment fund to "do good in the world." You are aware that 50 years ago, upon the death of our founder Paul Harris, The Rotary Foundation launched a scholarship program to enable promising young people to study abroad for one year. Some of you have participated in the cultural and humanitarian programs of The Rotary Foundation, which really began with *matching grants* in 1966 and blossomed with the Health, Hunger and Humanities grants in 1979.

So, today, I want to review a simple fact that there are two major parts of The Rotary Foundation. One side relates to the tremendous *programs* of The

Foundation; and the other side is the *fund-raising necessity* to pay for the programs. It is essential that all Rotarians understand and appreciate <u>both</u> parts of The Rotary Foundation.

The Rotary Foundation provides a window through which we can see a kaleidoscope of international programs promoting peace, goodwill and understanding. It is through this window Rotarians can see unusual opportunities for international service. Have you ever thought how your Rotary club could become involved in real international service projects if we did not have The Rotary Foundation? It is through this window of The Foundation that we can see the reality of the world.

Look through the window. Do you see the poverty which surrounds half the world's population? Can you see the millions of children who have no schools or educational opportunity? Do you see the people who are starving or live with chronic hunger? Do you see the children who are sick or crippled and the millions without any available medical care? Do you see the families who have no clean water to drink or safe sanitary conditions in which to live? Do you see the young people living on the streets of our cities and the people without shelter under which to sleep? Do you see the people caught in the web of drug and substance abuse and those who are physically and mentally abused? Do you see the men and women who have no jobs or no income to meet the basic needs of their families? Do you see those who live without hope or even a dream?

Look through the window! That's the real world. Oh, we can close the window. We can close our eyes. But, the problems will not go away.

Or, we can decide that Rotarians can build a better world through The Rotary Foundation. Those are our two options. In these most simple terms, that's the purpose of the programs of The Rotary Foundation – to meet educational and humanitarian needs of the world. By meeting these critical needs of the world and improving the quality of life, we strengthen the hope for world peace.

Have you ever seen The Rotary Foundation in action? Where malnutrition prevents normal growth in children, The Rotary Foundation is providing new sources of food and nutrition. Where water has been carried for generations from polluted streams, fresh water is pumped from Foundation funded wells. Where disease is rampant and useful life curtailed, The Foundation provides vans to bring vaccines, medical supplies and treatment. Where basic education is severely limited or non existent, The Foundation supports schools with books, equipment and teacher training. Where poverty stricken humans sleep on streets and in retched slums, The Foundation is building low-cost shelters. Where the environment has been spoiled by thoughtless destruction, The Foundation works to restore the air, water and natural resources. Where young students yearn for expanded educational opportunities., The Foundation provides scholarships for overseas studies, and unique Group Study Exchange team experiences.

It is almost impossible to imagine a humanitarian or educational opportunity which could not be addressed by our Rotary Foundation. The potential of The Rotary Foundation is limited only by the imagination of your district foundation committees. Innovative Rotarians throughout the world are the ones who create the amazing array of projects and programs of The

Rotary Foundation. All of these projects are created by your district and club committees which apply for a wide variety of grants and awards made by The Rotary Foundation.

At the present time, approximately 60% of the annual programs fund is expended to support educational programs and about 40% support humanitarian projects. If you think there should be more humanitarian grants, or more educational awards, your district can change those allocations. It is up to each district to determine the percentage of the funds which will be allocated to each part of the program. This is a very simple description of the annual programs of The Rotary Foundation.

Now, let's look at the other side of The Rotary Foundation – which we call Fund Development. You see, all of the wonderful Annual Programs of The Rotary Foundation depend each year upon one factor – the amount of money contributed to The Rotary Foundation.

We must remember that there will be no Ambassadorial Scholars, no matching grants, no 3-H grants, no volunteer programs, no cultural programs – until someone gives money to The Rotary Foundation.

Occasionally, a Rotarian will tell me, "Oh, I don't like to talk about raising money." What he or she may really be saying is, "I don't believe enough in the educational and humanitarian work of The Rotary Foundation to make the effort to see that the programs continue every year." If you honestly believe that the programs of The Rotary Foundation are worthwhile and important to the world, then you will naturally understand that they can only happen when the necessary funds are raised.

When you believe in The Rotary Foundation, you will give and you will work to see that the funds are raised every year. Generally speaking, people enjoy spending money more than they do raising it. But, just as we operate in our homes, businesses and professions, we can't spend money until we raise it. So, that is the reason that each Rotarian, each Rotary club and each district must consider raising funds a vital part of their duty and responsibility to support The Rotary Foundation to the best of their ability. But, the fact is, most people only give when they are specifically asked or motivated to do so.

How does your club support The Rotary Foundation? How can Rotarians be encouraged to do their share in the amazing work of The Foundation? Let me suggest a few ideas.

The first suggestion is to seek the participation of every Rotarian in every Rotary club. If you can achieve the objective of total involvement to the best level of each member's ability to give, we will go a long way toward reaching our annual goals. Consider this: a 100% club contribution to The Rotary Foundation is, in my opinion, just as important and probably more valuable, than 100% attendance at club meetings. Why not record that percentage of participation in the district governor's newsletter along with the attendance reports? Club leaders must talk about full participation of every member at every opportunity. Urge every member to make a personal contribution every year. The amount is not nearly as important as the full participation.

A second idea is to emphasize a small increase to the level of per capita giving to The Rotary Foundation each year. Last year (1997) the average per capita gift of all Rotarians in the world was about $65 dollars per person. Some districts were much higher and some were much lower. Take a look at your own club. Take a look at your own district. Then consider this: could our club increase our per capita contribution by five dollars; or ten dollars; or even twenty dollars?

You see, great achievements are not always made in giant leaps, but frequently by small incremental steps. If your club is one of those on the lower end of per capita giving, give some thought of how your club could just move up a little closer to the average of the Rotary world. If every Rotarian just gave a few more dollars per person, the results would be remarkable.

A third successful idea is the importance of encouraging and recognizing those who give gifts of $1000 or more. Since 1957, any individual who made a gift of $1000 has been recognized as a Paul Harris Fellow. In some instances, the gift may be made in the name of another person. The source of the funds makes no difference. The Paul Harris Fellow recognition is given as a sincere expression of appreciation by the Trustees of The Rotary Foundation for a gift of at least $1000.

At the present time, over 80% of all funds received by The Rotary Foundation are the result of these generous gifts by individuals. These gifts are absolutely vital to the success of the Annual Programs Fund. So, I encourage you to urge Rotarians in your clubs to make gifts in their own names, or in the name of a family member, an associate, friends, their Rotary sponsor, or a significant other – because that is the way your club can do your part in the worldwide work of Rotary. Never underestimate the value of sincere recognition and appreciation as a means to support The Rotary Foundation.

The fourth idea which is important in some areas of the world is to make gifts to the Permanent Fund of The Rotary Foundation. Although our primary task is to seek funds for the Annual Programs, some Rotarians have the financial ability and desire to give major gifts of perhaps $10,000 or more to the Permanent Fund, which will not be spent, but will be invested for future income. Others become "Benefactors" by making a gift to the Permanent Fund or a pledge of a substantial gift by bequest, wills or other financial plan.

In the years to come, the Permanent Fund will grow and earn millions of dollars in annual income to supplement and expand the work of The Rotary Foundation, to support new programs and meet the added costs of current activities. I anticipate that the Permanent Fund will exceed its target of $200 million by the 100th anniversary of Rotary. I dream of the time, somewhere in the future, when the Permanent Fund will surpass the billion dollar mark or maybe two billion. That is what I call a real dream for Rotary's future.

We have discussed the two sides of The Rotary Foundation – programs and fund development. One side is the glorious activities to enrich the lives of millions of people whom you may never meet or ever see, but Rotarians will always have the satisfaction of knowing that we are reaching out and touching the lives of people whose only hope is that there is someone who cares enough to help. The other side of fund development merely makes it possible for the programs to happen.

The Rotary Foundation is our window of opportunity. We must all work to keep that window open and to keep the fresh breezes of goodwill, understanding and concern for others invigorating our lives as Rotarians.

That second side of our Foundation is that very mundane fact of life – great programs require substantial sums of money each year to keep The Foundation alive. Our hands are the hands of The Rotary Foundation. If Rotarians are able to reach out with significant humanitarian and educational services, we must first reach deep into our own pockets and give generously to the level of our ability.

From this vantage point we can look out upon the world and realize that we have so much – and most of the world has so little.

A few months ago, I participated in the first National Immunization Day in Ethiopia. The president of that very poor country personally gave the first drops of polio vaccine to a long line of youngsters. As this was happening, there were about 35 youngsters on the side of the room in wheelchairs, leg braces or with crutches – all the tragic victims of polio. If we only had polio immunization two, four or five years earlier, these children would be able to walk, run and play as children ought to do. Then the 35 children stood up the best they could and sang a song to the President of their country. The song went something along this line: "It's too late for us, but don't let other children get polio. Please kick polio out of Africa."

Everyday, there are thousands of people who die from needless starvation and disease – and our wonderful Rotary programs are too late for them. Each night, millions of people are homeless and hopeless – and we are too late to show we care.

Oh, I wish all of you could have been there to hear the songs of those Ethiopian children – "It's too late for us – but do what you can to help others." And we are doing it through The Rotary Foundation.

Years ago, one man had a dream. It was the dream of an endowment fund to "do good in the world." We are doing good work in every part of the world. That is Rotary's great dream – which is coming true every day.

But there is so much more we can and must do. It is our task to keep that great dream alive through The Rotary Foundation. I'm confident that Rotarians can and will do it.

WHAT DID YOU LEARN?

(Over the years I have spoken at numerous college and university commencement ceremonies. This speech, which is similar to other addresses at graduation events, was delivered at the commencement of Heidelberg College on May 14, 1995.)

In the past forty years, I have probably attended two hundred commencement ceremonies. Frankly, I don't remember the words of even one commencement speaker. Commencements are one of the rituals of spring. Like wild flowers which burst forth with blooming platitudes. You never realize how little you know – until you begin preparing a speech for college seniors. But the *good* news is that I am not going to speak very long – but the *bad* news is, it will just seem long.

But first, let me say a special word to parents. This is your day, too. Thank you for helping these young men and women reach this high point in their lives. It is not easy to be a parent – especially when tuition bills come due. I suspect today some of you are thinking back to the days when these graduates were kids. You recall the taxi service you operated for Little League, ballet classes, 4-H, or the Scout troop. Some may be thinking back to the band concerts or piano recitals you sat through. Some may be recalling the endless ball games you endured. Do you remember those late nights when you waited for the sound of the family car turn into the driveway; or when an afternoon raid on the refrigerator consumed the entire family dinner; or your daughter declared she had nothing to wear to the big party – as she stood in front of a closet full of clothes? You see, these are often the memories recalled by parents who thought this day would never arrive. A few of you may have had serious doubts that their off-spring would ever "commence" doing anything. But today is that commencement day!

So, I express my sincerest congratulations to each parent, and grandparent, as well. This is your day to be very proud. And before this day is over, I hope each graduate, each in your way, will whisper to your parents, "Thanks for making this day possible."

Now, a word to the faculty is also appropriate. You are equally an important part of this day. You have touched the lives of these graduates and your influence continues to spread – as ripples on the waters – into all segments of society; into the business, professional, governmental, educational and family lives of these graduates. The influence of a teacher never ends. These graduates will move on from this campus – but teachers will stay – which is the nature of their calling. Next year a new group of young people will join the stream of students which will pass through the college. It has been said that a college is a storehouse of knowledge – because the freshmen bring so much in, and the seniors take so little away. But it is the faculty who place their mark and blessings on the graduates of 1995 – and for generations these future alumni will reflect and radiate the inspiration and challenge given by their dedicated mentors.

We must not forget the loyal administrators and staff members who have also contributed to this graduating class. These are the individuals who have worried about balancing budgets; maintaining the physical facilities; offering words of counseling; keeping records, renewing libraries and laboratories and providing all the other services which make a college appear to run itself. To President Cassell, I extend personal greetings and warmest good wishes.

Now, let me turn to the graduates and ask a basic question: "What did you learn?" Some of you may recall about 16 years ago when you trudged home from that first day at school, you were frequently asked, "What did you learn today?" I remember this was a favorite query of aunts, uncles and grandparents – who really don't know what to say to small children. As a child I always thought it was a dumb question. But at age five or six, it is difficult to distinguish between a rhetorical question and a dumb one. I recall one little tot, on his first day of school replied, "I don't know what I learned, but it wasn't enough, cause I have to go back tomorrow."

But, what *did* you learn these last four years? Some of you could eloquently discuss economic theories of the European Common Market; others might explain the evolutionary impact of South Pacific Ocean currents; of maybe the relative importance of cubit art; or hidden meanings in Shakespearean literature. Each in your own way has constructed a storehouse of facts, concepts and principles. You have been exposed to great ideas, challenging discussions and stimulating readings. Some of this specific knowledge you will long remember – but, much of it you will soon forget.

It is reported that students graduating with engineering and scientific degrees will find that half of what learned in college will be obsolete by the time they are thirty. Corporate employers point out that what an individual learns about a particular job is usually obsolete or incorrect in less than twenty years. To think of the possibility that half of the information or facts you have learned in these college years may be out-of-date in the foreseeable future is not a very rewarding prospect for four years of struggle and a $75,000 price tag.

But, take heart. There were many other things you learned which will stand the test of time.

The first lesson you may have learned was the necessity to accept personal responsibility. Thomas Huxley, the 19th Century British scientist and writer, stated: "Perhaps the most valuable of all education is to make yourself do the thing you have to do; when it ought to be done; whether you like it or not." Remember when you had to turn in that term paper to meet the deadline set by your professor? Remember when you had to read the book by Monday morning, when it was the weekend of the big dance or ball game? Remember, you practiced the concerto; repeated the laboratory experiment; took the examination – because it had to be done. As Dr. Huxley suggested, the vary act of finishing a task, whether you liked it or not, is in itself a symbol of the education process. The truly educated person completes any task – no matter how laborious or disagreeable – because it – because it needs to be done. Society needs and values those who accept difficult responsibilities and see that they are completed.

As I have traveled the world, I have seen men and women who willingly give their energy to build better communities. They tend the sick; feed the hungry; care for the poor; house the homeless; preserve the environment; teach the illiterate; and give hope to the hopeless. As a college graduate, you will be expected to do hundreds of things, just because they must be done. Some of these activities will be momentous. Many of you will serve in positions of leadership in your community and in the world. You will have high responsibilities thrust upon you.

But college graduates are also expected to do many simple tasks – most of which have little glamour or excitement. The world will expect you to get up in the morning and go to work. One of these days many of you will be transporting a carload of kids to a neighborhood swim meet, or summer camp; or attending PTA meetings; or collecting funds for the United Way, Cancer Society or a political campaign. You will be expected to serve on a school board or a civic committee, or organize the music for the Church Christmas pageant, or take part in a service club's community project. There are so many jobs which fall upon the shoulders of men and women who have learned to accept responsibility. That is your role in society. You are a college graduate. You have learned one of the most valuable lesson of education – to do the things you have to do when they ought to be done, whether you like it or not. I assure you that you will be a person sought out as worth knowing and relying upon throughout your lifetime.

WHAT DID YOU LEARN?

The second thing I hope you have learned in your years at Heidelberg is the personal pride which comes from excellence. Edwin Markham, the American poet, wrote the story of a young carpenter who was hired by a wealthy man to build a large home. The land owner said: "I've picked you because you're a good carpenter and I want the finest house ever built. It will be located up on that hill, and everyone will see it is the finest. Use all of the best materials and the most excellent workmanship available." The young carpenter eagerly took the job and was delighted to build such a beautiful house. Shortly afterwards, the land owner announced that he was taking a long journey, but hoped the house would be completed by the time he returned.

After the owner left the country, the young carpenter thought, "This is my chance to cut corners a little bit and make myself some extra money. So he started using second rate materials and the plumbing and electrical wiring "just got by." He knew the paint would cover all the inferior materials and the house would be so attractive that no one would ever know about the shoddy workmanship.

The beautiful new house was finished when the wealthy owner returned. The owner was delighted, so he called the young carpenter and said, "Young man, you've done an excellent job on my beautiful house. I like you very much. As you know, I am a very wealthy man and I have decided to offer you a present for all your effort. I'm going to give this house to you." Can you imagine the chagrin, disappointment and heartbreak of that young man when he realized that his new home was made of shoddy and second rate materials. All the time he had been cheating himself.

Each year at commencement time, I think about this story as I look into the eyes of each graduate. It is the story of a college experience. You often thought you were writing that term paper just for the professor; or doing homework for that teacher; or reading an assignment just to pass the class. But today, your professors are saying, "You've completed the job – and now the house belongs to you." I hope each of you is satisfied with the workmanship and the materials you put into your house. In the years ahead, if you ever think of doing less than your best – remember, the house may be given to you and you will be the first to feel the absence of real quality.

One of the great lessons of a Christian college is that personal pride and strength of character is usually built when we are alone. We experience the satisfaction of doing what is right or good for the sole reason that is right or good. We express the truth; we choose the honorable path – because truth and honor have proved to be the best guidelines for a rewarding life. If your college years have given you this insight, then you have truly had rewarding years at Heidelberg.

The third and final notion I hope you have learned is the value of lasting friendships. Each of you has met a host of new friends and acquaintances who will follow you for a lifetime. Some of these *friends* are the great scientists and philosophers whose research you have studied and debated. Artists, writers and composers of the ages have become your intimate *friends.* Your professors have introduced you to countless scholars and thinkers whose association you will increasingly value.

Equally important are your faculty friends, whose personal influence and indelible impressions you will carry with you. As the years pass, the gaps in age and distance between student and teacher tend to shrink and you will gradually realize that the relationship becomes that of colleagues and friends. Hold fast to that bond built on respect and intellectual appreciation, because your teachers will become some of your most rewarding and lasting friends.

Preserve also the rarest of all friendships – those you have made with your classmates. True college friendships are very precious. Some of the greatest blessings of life are friends with character and integrity you can count on, turn to, or completely trust. Throughout your lifetime you will meet many engaging, charming, talented, entertaining and colorful people. But, few will surpass the close friendships you have created in these past years with whom you can share confidences, who understand, who listen, who accept you, respect and provide the mutual strength on which lasting friendship is built. Those friends around you are priceless dividends of your college years.

There is a comment in Cicero's famous essay *On Friendship* which reads: "Without friendship there is no fullness of life, for if we lose affection and kindness from our life, we lose all that gives it charm." I hope each of you have found in this beautiful college the charm of friendship.

So, what did you learn? I hope you see the point I have been trying to make. Along with the facts and theories, you have learned other valuable lessons to make life meaningful and rewarding. I doubt that anyone will ever stop you on the street during your entire lifetime and ask you opinions about the relative merits of Doric and Corinthian columns. It would be amazing if someone chatted with you about the themes of *The Brothers Karamazov* or *The Life of Samuel Johnson*. Unless you are a contestant on the Jeopardy program – you may go through your entire life without having to recall the Babylonian Captivity, The Dreyfus Case, or Copernicus' Treatise on Heavenly Spheres. But the fact that these subjects are not part of daily discussion does not mean that are unimportant or to be relegated to useless tomes of trivia. The thousands of intellectual discoveries you have experienced are part of your fabric of life.

Yes, during these college days, you have learned many lessons – some technical and factual – but many are the practical experiences of life. In short, you have become an informed and responsible citizen ready to assume your role in whatever endeavor you choose.

I will close by recalling an old legend which tells of three housemen riding across an Eastern desert in the dark of night. As they crossed a dry bed of a river, a voice called out, "Halt." The three housemen drew up their horses as they were ordered. A voice from behind a clump of bushes continued, telling them to dismount, and pick up some pebbles and put them in their pockets. Then the strange voice declared, "You have done as I have commanded. Mount your horses and resume your journey. But remember, tomorrow at sunup, you will be both happy and sad."

The three men rode on, totally mystified at this strange encounter with a voice in the desert. At sunrise, they reached in their pockets, and were amazed to find that the pebbles were actually diamonds, rubies, emeralds and other precious gems. They were overjoyed. Then they recalled the warning the voice predicted – "At sunup you will be both happy and sad." And surely they were – happy that they had picked up the precious stones – but sad they had not taken more.

As you leave this beautiful campus, I suspect all of you are both happy and sad. You have pockets loaded with happy gems of knowledge, friendships and memories – but perhaps a little sad that you could not have selected even more.

What did you learn? Oh, so many things. You came to learn – now go into your future. Go forth and serve your family, your profession, your community and the world. Treasure the pebbles you take with you. Among them are many lessons – and even many you never realized you learned.

Congratulations and Godspeed in the years ahead.

PRESIDENTIAL MINUTES

[These short articles were written and given to Rotary club presidents to use as informational and motivational messages at club meetings and also to be used as occasional items for club newsletters.]

WHAT IS ROTARY?

Occasionally, people will ask, "What Is Rotary?" There is a fairly simple description that we can use. "Rotary is a service organization of business and professional leaders, united worldwide, who help those in need, encourage high ethical standards in all vocations and work toward world understanding and peace." That one long sentence describes pretty much what our organization is all about. You could put it another way and merely say, "Rotarians are community leaders who meet weekly to enjoy a lot of fun and fellowship, and then do things to build a better community and serve others at home and around the world." Rotary is the world's most international organization. It was the first service club. We help the poor, the disabled, the underprivileged, the hungry, the homeless, the illiterate, and the hopeless through a wide variety of humanitarian and educational programs. That is why we are proud to be Rotarians.

FRIENDSHIP

Do you have any friends? That might seem like a funny question to ask. Most of us have some friends, unless we are a recluse or hermit. But, I raise the question merely to ask if you are really taking advantage of the opportunities that we have in our Rotary club to build lasting friendships. Oliver Wendell Holmes wrote: "There is no friend like an old friend who has shared one's morning day; no greeting like his welcome; no homage like his praise." We all enjoy old friends. But, old friends are not made in a hurry. If you would like to have such friends in the years to come, each of us should start making new friends now. Sturdy friends, like sturdy beams, take time to season. Rotary gives us that opportunity to select persons we feel pretty sure could be the kind of friends we could prize in future years. I hope all of you are using these opportunities to start that gentle, gradual, seasoning process – to find and eventually become an *old Rotary friend*. That is one of the rewards of being a Rotarian.

NEW YEAR RESOLUTIONS

As we begin a new year, it is traditional that some resolutions are made. As we enter the New Year, how about considering this resolution list as a responsible Rotarian?

- I will find a person or two who should be a member of our club and bring them as a guest to our meetings.

- I am going to spend just a few minutes each week chatting with two members with whom I usually have no contact, just to expand my circle of friends.

- I am going to see if there is a committee, which needs my personal service.

- I am going to have a totally new Rotary experience by attending the Rotary International Convention in June.

- I am going to become more involved in the club meeting each week with some *high fives* and *happy bucks* because good things are happening in my life and I wish to share the news.

And if you make, and keep, these resolutions, you will enjoy the privilege of being a Rotarian even more in the coming year. So, Happy New Year!

ROTARY'S GIFT TO YOU

Have you ever stopped to think exactly what you might personally receive just because you are a member of this Rotary club? There are many rewards, if we look for them. Rotary brings us once a week into close contact with a cross-section of our community. Our weekly programs keep us more aware and, thus, more interesting persons. Rotary gives us information and viewpoints on many issues which face our state, nation and the world through interesting speakers and programs. Rotary gives us opportunities to be of service to others, and thus find certain satisfaction in showing our compassion for those less fortunate than we. Rotary gives us a special kind of good fellowship and fun, which is stimulated by an association with interesting and lasting friends. Rotary gives a rewarding dimension to our lives, which can make us better individuals. Sometimes when we look around, we realize that Rotary gives us much more than we ever expected.

DO YOU EVER EXPRESS APPRECIATION?

The ancient scriptures tell of ten lepers who were cured of that dreaded disease. However, only one returned to give thanks. I hope contemporary ingratitude isn't as high as 90 percent. Nevertheless, far too many of us never bother to give thanks when it is so well deserved. Each week we come to our Rotary meeting and are so used to expecting good speakers and entertaining programs that we frequently fail, or perhaps just forget, to express our appreciation in any way to our program speakers. We have outstanding programs at our Rotary club. And even occasionally we will have a really grand slam homerun! Why not stop a moment and say a sincere word of "thanks" to our speakers. Real gratitude and appreciation is a feeling which should not be concealed. Just saying, "Thanks for taking your time to come to our Rotary club," is a thoughtful way to let our speakers know that we appreciate the time, money, effort and willingness to contribute freely to our Club. Start a new habit. One word of "thanks" which is actually spoken or written is worth a thousand kind and wonderful thoughts you had, but never expressed.

ROTARY FRIENDSHIPS

Do you realize that one of the nicest things about Rotary is the friendships we create? When we join a Rotary club we may know one or two members. But week after week, deep and lasting friendships develop. Casual acquaintances sometimes grow into some the closest friends we ever have. I think this happens in Rotary because you can just be yourself. There are no formalities in Rotary. First names are the tradition. We don't address each other with titles of "doctor," "mister," or other formality. We accept each other as equals. We exchange greetings, joke, kid each other, and just create a relationship, which only real friends can have. We care about each other, our families, our vocations, our achievements and our disappointments. That's what we mean by *The Family of Rotary*. I hope that each member is experiencing some of these unique rewards of Rotary. Our club is a great place to build new friendships.

WHO WILL BENEFIT?

An ancient story is told of the great Roman Emperor Hadrian who found an aging man planting olive trees, and since they grow so slowly, he said: "Old man, these trees will not bear fruit for many years. Do you expect to be alive to eat the fruit of your labor?" The old man replied, "If God wills, I shall eat – and if not, my son will eat. My father and his father before him planted trees that I might have fruit. It is my duty, then, to provide for those who shall come after me." This is the story of human progress. We plant trees, cultivate ideas, extend knowledge, and build a better community – not just for ourselves, but for those who come after us. Our forefathers cultivated great ideas in building this nation and our community. Let us never forget that it is our responsibility to cultivate what we have inherited, and to plant trees for those who will someday enjoy the fruit.

TIME IS WASTING

How many times have you said, "I'll do that tomorrow?" And tomorrow comes and goes, and our good intentions pass away. Stephen Grellet wrote many years ago an article called "Do It Now" with these words: "I expect to pass through this world but once. Any good thing, therefore, that I can do, or any kindness that I can show a fellow being, let me do it now. Let me not defer or neglect it, for I shall not pass this way again." This is a message for all of us. So often all the fine things we intended to do, and say, and give, and support, and love and serve and be, are just not accomplished in 24 hours. Let's not forget that just little random acts of kindness are special kinds of Rotary Service. Why not do it today? Call a friend you haven't talked to for some time. Stop and visit a person who might be pleased to see you. Tell someone you care about them. Go out of your way to help someone who may need you. That's what Rotary's motto – Service Above Self – really means. Service doesn't have to be a big deal – little things can be huge to a friend or neighbor. Remember – "We shall not pass this way again."

INVITE A FRIEND TO ROTARY

Have you ever stopped to think what outstanding pro-grams we have each week in our Rotary club? We have had some excellent speakers talking and inform-ing us about our community, interesting state and na-tional issues, and some of the significant work of Ro-tary in the world. It is rather sad that we are not sharing these messages with ten or a dozen other friends and community leaders. We could easily accommodate a dozen more guests each week – but you have to invite them. Invite your accountant, minister, attorney, dentist or neighbor to come to Rotary. Maybe even your broth-er-in-law or spouse would find the program of special interest. The door is open every week – think about it – bring a guest. If they realize what an enjoyable event

Rotary can be each week, they might even want to become a member. Who will be your guest next week?

THE MESSAGE OF SERVICE

A story is told about a group of radio operators who were being interviewed for a job with a big steamship company. They were all gathered in a busy office and there was noise of excited talk, phones ringing, and lots of dots and dashes on a loudspeaker system. No one was paying much attention to the noise and confusion. Suddenly, one fellow in the corner snapped to his feet and walked though the door marked *Private Office*. A few minutes later he came out smiling. He had the job. "Hey," called out one of the group, "How did you get in there ahead of us, we were here first?" "One of you could have had the job," he replied, "If you had listened to the message." "What message?" they all asked. "Why, the code message on the loud speaker. We are all radio operators and anyone could have heard the code spell out, 'The man who gets this message and comes directly into my private office will be placed on one of my ships as the radio operator." The one, who got the message, got the job. In Rotary, the *message of service* is coming across loud and clear and it is our task to hear and recognize it. There are jobs to do, projects to start, and tasks to complete. But, these things only happen if our club stands up when we hear the *message of service*.

ACTIONS ARE WHAT COUNT

Someone once wrote, "Even a fair idea – put to use – is better than a great idea kept in the file." I have heard dozens of ideas of what our club or Rotary International ought to do to help people in our community or around the world. Yes, there are many ideas of things we could do, but the only ones which really count are those which we are willing to do. Progress is made by *actions,* not just by suggestions, ideas or intentions. A small job, which we actually did, is far better than a huge task we intended to do. To be a Rotarian is to serve. And "service" is a word of action. All tasks are not huge or earth shaking, but they can be important in the lives of some individual. There are many lists of great projects a Rotary club can undertake, but the only ones which really count, are those which we actually begin and complete.

THE RULE OF THE WOOD PILE

There is a saying, which developed on the old camping trails, which admonishes the outdoorsman to "always leave the wood pile a little higher than when you found it." Any camper or woodsman knows that rule is a good one. We can use and enjoy the campsite and natural resources of the area, but we have an obligation to those who come after us to provide the same privileges and pleasures. In Rotary, too, each of us has a responsibility to share Rotary and build the membership just a little higher. There is no Rotary club which could not benefit from an increase of several worthy and deserving members. The real purpose for Rotary membership growth is to provide more hands to do the work of service and more friends to share the special fellowship of Rotary. Let's not forget the rule of the woodpile, "Leave a little more than when you found it."

WE CAN ALL DO SOMETHING

A room may be dark because the sun is not shining. Or, the room may be dark because the windows are dirty.

What can you do? Of course, you can't turn on the sun – but you can wash the windows. In our <u>Rotarian Magazine</u>, we frequently read about the amazing acts of humanitarian service some people are doing around the world. Most of us can't do those fantastic things. But, there is no reason to become discouraged by the jobs we can't do – just do the jobs we can. Here in our own community there are people who need friendship, acts of kindness, and a little personal attention. We can do that. There are children who need the support and caring of the adult community. We can do that. We have a community, which needs civic leaders. We can do that. In our Rotary club, let's do the jobs we *can do*, and not worry too much about the things for which we have little control.

ENJOY OUR WEEKLY MEETINGS

Is there any way that our weekly Rotary club meetings could be even more enjoyable? Let me suggest a few ideas: First, arrive at the meeting just a few minutes early and enjoy a little more conversation and fellowship. Give a sincere greeting to as many members as you can. Make a point of getting acquainted with one of our new members. Introduce yourself to a visitor who might be visiting our club for the first time. After the program, stop a moment to give a word of thanks and appreciation to the speaker. Take your time on the way out to say a few "good-byes." As you go on your way you might wonder why that Rotary meeting was a little bit better than any other you have ever attended. Try it. You'll be pleased to realize how good our Rotary club's meetings really are when you follow a few easy steps.

A ROTARY DISTRICT CONFERENCE

Some Rotarians think that a District Conference is just for the club officers and district leaders. No way! The Conference is for all Rotarians and their spouses. For new members, a District Conference gives an insight into the activities that make Rotary such a fine organization. It will make you proud to be a member. For the time-tested Rotarians, the Conference is a must. You will surely meet some friendly members from other clubs. There will be some interesting talks and presentations. You probably will participate in some stimulating discussions, and enjoy a few laughs and a lot of fun. For the spouses, they too will enjoy the program, the social activities, and maybe just a different kind of weekend outing. For everyone, the District Conference will be an inspiring and memorable event. It is Rotary at its very best. So, why not plan to join us and find how much fun it can be.

DIFFERENCES OF OPINION

Once in a while we may have speakers or programs, which have a message with which everyone would not agree. A Rotary club meeting is not a sounding board for political promoters, eccentric economists or screwball philosophers, but they sometimes edge in under false pretenses, which is an understandable hazard when we seek interesting topics and unpaid speakers. Frankly, it usually doesn't do much harm and if you are totally bored, you can count the light bulbs on the chandelier. It certainly indicates that if you attend Rotary programs long enough there will probably be a few programs with which you can't agree or have very little interest. If you are not interested in the history of lace making or North Atlantic tidal waves, just sit back and mentally plan your shopping list. One thing about Rotary is that we can occasionally disagree – but hopefully it is not in a disagreeable manner.

VOCATIONAL SERVICE

One of the four points in the Object of Rotary is *Vocational Service.* Vocational Service means, in part, valuing a person's worth by the service he or she performs. The question of a person's worth is not determined by a whim or benevolence of the employer – but by what service they perform. A cartoon pictures a bar of iron worth $10. The same bar of iron, made into horseshoes would be worth $25. Made into needles, it has a value of $5,000; and if turned into balance springs for fine watches, it becomes worth $500,000. The value of any material is not determined so much from what it is made, as by the service it performs. The same seems true with people. That's why Rotarians believe *Vocational Service* is a valuable object of Rotary. It describes the service we perform in our business and professional life.

THE "YOU" IN ROTARY

If our Rotary club were to disappear tomorrow, would anyone miss it? If Rotary International were to disappear tomorrow, would anyone notice? The answer, for Rotarians, comes when we ask ourselves, "What have I done in the past 6 months to benefit our Rotary club? What has our club done for our community in the last 3 months? What would become of our club if every member had done about as much as I have done? What would happen if no member invited a guest to become a new member?" Rotary is a personal thing. If you take pride in our club, and give some of your personal time, thought, effort, and energy, then our club will be much stronger and more valuable to our community. Remember – *You* are Rotary.

EXPAND OUR ROOTS

A Japanese bonsai tree is a living miniature of the full-grown tree, but it is kept dwarfed by not allowing its roots to spread. A bonsai tree is a thing of beauty, but always bound in size by its limited root system. A full sized tree digs its roots into the earth and spreads its root system seeking nourishment, and its limbs and vegetation spread accordingly. Rotary is quite the same. The club that keeps its roots confined and bound offers little, except, perhaps a beautiful appearance. However, the club that spreads its roots into the whole community is the club that can spread its benefits as widely as its root system. It is important that our Rotary club spreads our roots throughout the community, by expanding our membership.

A FRIENDLY ROTARY CLUB

What kind of welcome do visitors receive at our club? A few years ago, the West Hollywood Rotary Club decided that they would be the "friendliest Rotary club in the world." Here is the set of principles they announced:

- By treating each visiting Rotarian as an honored guest and not as an unfortunate accident washed upon our shore at lunchtime.

- By seating visitors at different tables instead of clustering visitors and guests at just one table.

- By having their own club members seated beside each guest and introduce them around the table.

- By seeing that no visitor ever has an empty seat besides him or her, by assuring that their own members filled in empty spaces.

- By treating each visitor or guest to the club as we would if they were a visitor in our own homes.

How does our club match up with these criteria? A great Rotary club is a very friendly club – for both our own members and for visitors and guests.

THE HARMONY OF ROTARY

Have you ever watched the tuba player in a German Band? He just plays, oomph-paw-paw, oomph-paw-paw, with no harmony at all. If everyone just played the same notes, there wouldn't be much of a musical performance. But each instrument has its own part to play, and it is blended into beautiful harmony. A Rotary club is similar to the musical group – each member has a special part to play, if we expect harmonious music. There is a part for everyone in our Rotary club, whether large or small. The true spirit of a good harmonious Rotary club is when each member plays his or her part – even if you are just the oomph-paw-paw of the tuba player. We always need cornets, trombones and a couple violins. Which part are you playing?

SERVICE ABOVE SELF

Rotary's motto, *Service Above Self*, is worth reviewing from time to time. When we give *service* we sometimes think we know exactly what the other person needs. But we later find out that we did not understand their true needs. It is far better to help people help themselves, than merely meeting a need for someone else that we think is important. Secondly, service must not degrade the recipient, by making the receiver feel obliged or considered a pauper. When you help others to retain their own dignity and worth, you will have provided an even greater service than if you had only clothed and fed them. Finally, service must be *above* self. There is always the subtle danger that we make others feel an obligation, or that we become indispensable to others and leave them in a position of dependency upon us. Service Above Self is a wonderful motto, but we must exercise it with thoughtfulness and caring.

THE ROTARY WHEEL

We see the Rotary Wheel on our literature, our pin, our meeting banners and flags. Did you ever stop to think what that wheel means? The Rotary Wheel is unique. It has no rim; it has no tire; it cuts no ruts; it makes no squeak. The Rotary Wheel just rolls silently along. The wheel identifies Rotary service wherever you find it. It welcomes fellow Rotarians as they visit other communities. It is a symbol which calls thousands to the weekly meetings – just for an hour or so retreat from work and tensions. It appeals to the heart and minds of a million men and women who believe that service to others is a worthwhile endeavor. The Rotary Wheel often is a mark of miracles performed in a far off land. To a Rotarian, the pin with the Rotary Wheel is a symbol of distinction. I hope you wear your pin regularly with that kind of pride.

ROTARY PUBLIC RELATIONS

Every Rotary club needs to tell the public what Rotary is and what Rotary does. A Rotary club without an active public relations program is like winking at a pretty girl in the dark. We know what we are doing, but no one else does. No Rotarian should ever hesitate to tell others what our Rotary club does, or to bring a guest to our meetings. We do many things for our community and we reach around the world to assist those who live in poverty conditions. If we don't let the public know what Rotary service means, qualified men and women will never be attracted of join Rotary. It is both an opportunity and a responsibility for each of us to tell the story of Rotary to our friends and associates throughout the community.

THE VALUE OF FELLOWSHIP

It has been said that "fellowship" is the lubricant of service. But even a well-oiled mechanism has no usefulness if it doesn't operate. A Rotary club, worthy of the name, represents men and women who sense that the congenial association of our weekly meetings and social events are just the beginning of our activities of service. When there is a job to do, you seldom call on strangers. No, you call on those friends whom you know will gladly assist. So, it is important that we keep the wheels of Rotary fellowship well oiled in our club, if our acts of service are to be expanded throughout the community. Yes, Rotary has two important elements – fellowship and service.

INTERNATIONAL SERVICE

There are so many people in the world who live in poverty, ignorance and hopelessness. That is why our club looks beyond our borders and across the oceans for opportunities to help someone, somewhere. The urgent needs of the world are almost unlimited. "We live in a world which is full of misery and ignorance," said Thomas Huxley, the British scientist and educator, "And the plain duty of each and every one of us is to make the little corner of our influence somewhat less miserable and somewhat less ignorant than it was before we entered." We certainly can't minister to all the tragedies of the world, but each Rotary club can reach out is some way to *do something, for someone, somewhere.* That's what international service means.

PROPOSING A NEW MEMBER

One of the great privileges each of us can enjoy, as a member of Rotary is the right to propose a new member. That privilege will also give the new member the opportunity to enjoy all the pleasures that Rotary offers. The reason many good people are not Rotarians is simply – *nobody ever asked them.* Think of all the business establishments, the professions, and the community leaders in our community who are not represented in our club, just because they have never been invited to join. We all remember the person who sponsored us into Rotary. You, too, will always be remembered if you invite a fine citizen of our community to become a Rotarian.

ROTARY IS BIG IN THE WORLD

Rotary International is the oldest movement of its kind in the world and the most international organization of men and women who share a belief in good fellowship and service. This fact adds a certain dignity and prestige to Rotary which other similar organizations can never attain. Thus, Rotary means something *big* in the world. So, to be a member of Rotary should mean something *big* in the life of each individual who has the privilege of being a Rotarian. Have you ever stopped to consider what an honor it is to belong to such a distinguished and prestigious international organization? If it means something big to you – why not share it with another worthy friend?

ABOUT THE AUTHOR

Clifford L. Dochterman, Sr. served as worldwide President of Rotary International in 1992-93. For over 50 years, he has served in almost every Rotary assignment in the world, from President of the Berkeley, California Rotary Club, District Governor of District 5160, Rotary International Director in 1983-85, Vice President of Rotary International, and Trustee of The Rotary Foundation from 1993 to 1999.

His professional career included over 45 years in higher education administration, which included 20 years each at the University of California at Berkeley, and the University of the Pacific in Stockton.

Cliff has had a lifetime association with the Boy Scouts of America and has received three of their highest awards – Silver Beaver, Silver Antelope and Distinguished Eagle.. He has been president of the local Chamber Of Commerce and chairman of the county Parks and Recreation Commission. His speeches have been recognized by the Freedoms Foundation of Valley Forge by the George Washington Honor Medal.

It has been said that Cliff has spoken to more Rotary Clubs than anyone in the world. He is the author of the book, "ABCs of Rotary," and numerous educational monographs. He was one of the pioneers of Rotary's Polio Plus program which is eradicating the disease of polio in the world. He has chaired nearly every forward looking Rotary planning committee in the past 25 years.

Cliff and his wife, Mary Elena, belong to the Rotary Club of Moraga, near San Francisco, California. Mary Elena is also a past Rotary club president and a recipient of Rotary's Service Above Self Award.

Made in the USA
Lexington, KY
17 June 2011